The Race For Riches

The Race for Riches:

The Human cost of wealth

JEREMY SEABROOK

Marshall
Pickering

Green print
Marshall Pickering
3 Beggarwood Lane, Basingstoke, Hants RG23 7LP, UK

First published in 1988 by Marshall Morgan and Scott
Publications Ltd
Part of the Marshall Pickering Holdings Group
A subsidiary of the Zondervan Corporation

ISBN 1 85425 003 5

Text Set in Sabon 11/12 by Input Typesetting Ltd, London
Printed in Great Britain by Cox and Wyman, Reading

Contents

Contents

Some parts of this book have appeared as articles in *The Guardian*, *The Independent*, *New Statesman* and *Resurgence*. I am grateful to the editors for permission to republish here.

Jeremy Seabrook, July 1988

Introduction

That the greatest hope for the abolition of poverty was for so long placed in the productive power of the capitalist economy can now be seen to have been an illusion; and a costly, prolonged illusion at that. Poverty is essential to the purposes of capitalism: not only does it act as a spur to ever more intensive accumulation, but it is also an inescapable by-product of a zero-sum process, whereby the gains of some are always at the expense of others, however remote these may be from the point of production. Indeed, in recent years, dissimulating the relationship between producers and consumers, between the makers of primary products and the users of them has become a major source of employment in the rich Western economies.

In the early days of industrial society, natural scarcity — so long the experience of the majority of humankind — could be invoked to demonstrate the need for untrammelled economic growth. With the vast enhancement of the capacity to produce in the twentieth century, this is scarcely credible now. What has happened in the period sometimes called late capitalism (an unfortunate term, for it suggests that capitalism may be defunct or at least tottering towards its ruin, and whatever else it may be, it certainly isn't that) is that human beings have been systematically impoverished in ways that would make them more or less receptive to capitalist 'answers' to the new forms of poverty thus created. Indeed, there has been no limit to the resources that have been invested in the maintenance of poverty. Poverty, artificially induced, scrupulously perpetuated, is one of the more remarkable artefacts in a breathtaking range of contemporary products. What makes it even more extraordinary is that this poverty has been created out of the very mechanism which was to have assured the people's emancipation from it — the creation of wealth. For as money and what it can buy slowly colonizes greater and greater areas of our daily experience, this is accompanied by a growing dependency upon it. As faith in money grows, faith in ourselves and in each other decays. With time, even the memory of non-monetized ways of answering human need fades and dies, and money becomes the sole enabling agent of increasing areas of human activity. As long as individuals continue to enjoy a rising income, the true nature of this process remains veiled and the deepening dependency and accompanying depowerment are not perceived for what they are. Even though it is quite common to hear people say 'You can't do anything without money', the implications of this awesome development are still not recognized. Yet it is this violent process and the subordination of people to it that makes of poverty such an appalling visitation, even in the richest societies in the world.

It is this imperfectly understood dynamic that underlies the Green critique of industrial society, a critique that extends also to those socialist political formations that do not question the need for unlimited economic growth but merely plan to divert that growth to more humane ends.

If the creation of wealth itself destroys and wastes humanity, that wealth, however vast, will never suffice to repair the ravages it has wrought; and it is this contradiction that has done so much to damage the ambitions of socialists in the contemporary world. Money cannot cure what money has caused.

It is clear to many people that the model of industrial society, both capitalist and existing socialist, involves the most systematic squandering of human resources as it mounts its predatory assault on the resources of the earth.

Indeed, they are part of a single, symbiotic process. In order to pave the way for the latter, the human resources — the creativity, ingenuity, hopeful effort and self-reliance — must first be depleted, used up and extinguished. The forms of poverty thus produced will then appear to be remedied by an industrial expansion that, in turn, uses up, depletes and exhausts the natural riches of the world. To prise apart this powerful dynamic is the most urgent task for any politics that is serious about contesting the present immobilism and impotence of most contemporary moral and political discussion. The Green project is the only one that even takes cognizance of these forms of violence in the world. If it fails to illuminate our understanding of processes that simultaneously gut human beings and eviscerate the planet itself, no other politics . will.

This book is an attempt to illustrate the kind of impoverishment that occurs in the presence of unexampled wealth, in both the rich societies, and what is more obvious, in the poorer ones. It will also look at where resistance to such developments is coming from; and how such resistance may be strengthened, so that the whole process may be halted and, one day, reversed, in ways that will not frighten or alarm people, but that will appear to them as an emancipation from their fearful and threatening dependency.

We are confronting a constant and relentless pauperization of our humanity in the name of wealth-creation. This is an expropriation, not merely of our labour, but of deeper things, of our ability to lead our own lives, to deal with our own feelings, to trust our own perceptions, our own experience of living and suffering, of celebrating and of dying. This process of immiserating dependency on money, because at first it seems adequately to compensate for the forfeited substance of our lives, is not felt for the addiction it is. Only when it is far advanced and we can see there is no going back are we able to measure our loss of power and control. Abject and impotent without our enabling supply of money (that death-dealing life-support system), it is a more than linguistic irony that those considered to be 'independent' or 'of independent means' are in fact pioneers of this race towards depowerment and loss.

Many people in the West have become uneasily aware that a moment of reckoning must come. Indeed, there is a widespread feeling that it can't go on like this indefinitely; yet few have much idea how such a day of (strictly secular) judgment may be avoided. This is why there is so much rhetoric about the future, entering the twenty-first century, the hopes for our children's children: it is to conceal and compensate for the fact that we are living in and for the moment, not really thinking or caring about those who will come after us at all. The incantations about a better world for our children merely suppress the disturbing idea that our legacy to them will be an inheritance of nightmarish and intractable horror. For there exists already, inscribed in the collective imagination of the world, a powerful image of the total wreck of both humanity and our home in the world; and that is the pervasive image of nuclear annihilation. What makes this even more terrifying is that it represents a more immediate and cataclysmic version of something that is actually occurring here and now, little by little, in our daily practice. Nuclear extinction may be understood as an intensification, a disastrous and instantaneous acceleration of a ruinous process that is already in train, although more gradual, more insidiously stealthy, although dissimulated or denied by those in power. The reason why the prospect of nuclear destruction frightens so many people is not because the equilibrium of nuclear deterrence may break down, but rather because it actually makes concrete something which, at one level, we know to be happening already. It merely embodies what is already shadowed in the way we live, and *in the consequences for the world of that way of living*. It can be glimpsed in those images of spectral leafless forests; of dust-bowls and deserts that follow in the wake of deforestation; the receding water tables and the rains that fail; of dispossessed peasants and farmers abandoning their blighted lands and going to squat in the spreading megacities with their acres of slum settlements; of the exhaustion and depletion of a once-nourishing earth, while the rich look for ever new ways of spending their money that can only accelerate the cycle of impoverishment. For the rich eat up the substance of the poor at the same time as they seek more elaborate forms of escape from their own inner desolation — that mirror of the tormented and ruined landscape without.

In this context, the Green endeavour is not some marginal or minority preoccupation. It is caught up with our survival; and it offers hope not simply to the poor, but to all whose instinct for life prevails over the death-wish that feeds existing patterns of development. For present forms of wealth-creation impoverish not only those who are exploited by them, but equally those who are enriched; and they menace us all with the ultimate impoverishment.

CHAPTER ONE

The cost of wealth

All the countries in the world are developing countries; there is no such thing as a developed country, for that would suggest that all clocks can be stopped; it implies an extra-historical finality that is not vouchsafed us on earth. The use of the word *developed* to indicate the rich Western countries is an ideological one. It gives illusions of stability and permanence, and distracts from the fact that restlessness, change and violent discontinuities are the forces that govern these societies, as they have done since the beginning of the industrial era.

Development in this context means essentially the breaking of sustainability, the ending of dependency upon the renewable resources of the earth — what was once triumphantly hailed as 'the conquest of nature.' The costs of this rupture with sustainable practice have had to be borne by nature itself. This may perhaps be regarded as a kind of revenge for an antique human subservience to the tyranny of climate and season, drought and flood, famine and feast. The liberatory impulse of industrialism offered such extraordinary promises of wealth that it was at first little doubted that nature would easily absorb whatever violence might be inflicted upon it in the process. Having always been the supreme arbiter of human destiny, any partial escape from its constraints could only be emancipatory: what we are being liberated from is always more certain than what we are being liberated into.

The exultation of those dominators of nature was boundless. Even the most fierce critics of the capitalist endeavour, including Marx, denounced only the human consequences for the exploited, and had nothing but admiration for the productive powers released by bourgeois society. In a famous passage in the Communist Manifesto, he says

> 'The bourgeoisie, during its rule of scarce one hundred years, has created more massive and more colossal productive forces than have all preceding generations together. Subjection of Nature's forces to man, machinery, application of chemistry to industry and agriculture, steam-navigation, railways, electric telegraphs, clearing of whole continents for cultivation, canalisation of rivers, whole populations conjured out of the ground — what earlier century had even a presentiment that such productive forces slumbered in the lap of social labour? . . . [The bourgeoisie] has been the first to show what man's activity can bring about. It has accomplished wonders far surpassing Egyptian pyramids, Roman aqueducts, and Gothic cathedrals; it has conducted expeditions that put in the shade all former Exoduses of nations and crusades.'

An argument that long predates industrialism is more sharply focused from the eighteenth century — whether the energies released by unbridled human desire are a creative or destructive force in the world. What had earlier been a moral or spiritual question, at the time of the industrial revolution became a battle over whether human domination of the natural world was an act of hubris, or whether, on the contrary, the forms of progress it made possible meant the end of age-old poverty and subordination. Long before Marx's paean of praise to the power of capitalism to produce (an enthusiasm which has cost the world dear), Rousseau had warned, in his *Discourse on the Origins of Inequality among Men*, that 'Man has hardly any troubles except those he has given himself . . . It is only with great effort that we have managed to make

ourselves unhappy. When on the one hand one considers
the immense works of man, so many sciences brought to
perfection, so many arts invented, so many forces turned
to use, abysses filled in, mountains raised, rocks broken,
rivers made navigable, lands cleared, lakes dug out,
marshes drained, enormous buildings reared on the earth,
the sea covered with ships and sailors; and when on the
other hand one looks with a little reflection for the real
advantages resulting from all this for the happiness of the
human race, one can only be struck by the astonishing
disproportion between the two, and lament the blindness
of man, who, to feed his pride and I know not what vain
self-admiration, chases so eagerly after all the miseries he
is prey to, which beneficent nature had taken care to keep
from him . . . With man in society, first it is a question of
acquiring what is necessary, then what is superfluous; then
come luxuries, then immense riches; then subjects and
then, slaves; he has not a moment's respite.'

The critique of industrialism was always a dual one —
on the one hand the damage it inflicted upon the workers,
and on the other, the violation of nature. Although seen
as aspects of the same process, the argument remained a
moral one, at least until Marx's sulphurous predictions of
the consequences of the necessary immiseration of the
proletariat; and even then, it was not doubted that nature
could continue to absorb indefinitely the ravages that the
creation of wealth would inflict. Thus, Wordsworth, in
The Excursion, 1814, on the growth of manufacturing
cities:

" . . . I grieve when on the darker side
Of this great change I look; and there behold
Such outrage done to nature as compels
The indignant power to justify herself;
Yea, to avenge her violated rights,
For England's bane. — When soothing darkness spreads
O'er hill and vale', the Wanderer thus expressed
His recollections, 'and the punctual stars,

While all things else are gathering to their homes,
Advance, and in the firmament of heaven
Glitter — but undisturbing, undisturbed;
As if their silent company were charged
With peaceful admonitions for the heart
Of all-beholding Man, earth's thoughtful lord;
Then, in full many a region, once like this
The assured domain of calm simplicity
And pensive quiet, an unnatural light
Prepared for never-resting Labour's eyes
Breaks from a many-windowed fabric huge;
And at the appointed hour a bell is heard,
Of harsher import than the curfew-knoll
That spake the Norman Conqueror's stern behest —
A local summons to unceasing toil!
Disgorged are now the ministers of day;
And, as they issue from the illumined pile,
A fresh band meets them, at the crowded door —
And in the courts — and where the rumbling stream,
That turns the multitude of dizzy wheels,
Glares, like a troubled spirit, in its bed
Among the rocks below. Men, maidens, youths,
Mother and little children, boys and girls,
Enter, and each the wonted task resumes
Within this temple, where is offered up
To Gain, the master idol of the realm,
Perpetual sacrifice.'

It is not difficult to understand why protests against the
spoliation of nature became secondary: the more urgent
issue of the existence of a menacing mass of poor and
working-class people overshadowed what was considered
a mere question of aesthetics. The internal threat to the
growth and well-being of industrial society eclipsed what
were seen as sentimental regrets over the impairment of
the natural world. And with time, the sense of exile from
the countryside, the loss of contact with nature, became
more or less easily sublimated in the licensed nostalgias of

9

the culture; a development which persists to this day, when a rural fantasy is exploited both by the advertising industry, and by estate agents selling a functionless and suburbanized village life to refugees from the towns.

For the most part, all political preoccupation was focused on the question of the working class, and the capacity of capitalism to raise them up, attach them to itself or risk being overthrown.

Of course, the other argument was only submerged by what seemed more pressing concerns with the condition of the people in the dangerous and unwholesome environment of the industrial areas; it certainly didn't die. Throughout the late nineteenth century and the first half of the twentieth, the opponents of an industrialism that rested increasingly upon the abuse of the earth that ultimately nurtured it kept up a vigorous and passionate criticism of agricultural practice that sacrificed the long-term health of the land to short-term profit. R.H.Elliott in *Agricultural Changes* in 1898 was warning even then that 'the chemist with his artificial manures can only provide a costly chemical agent which must always be at the mercy of the season, and not only cannot permanently ameliorate the fertility of the soil, even in the most favourable seasons, but, unless supported by dung and turf, must deplete the soil'. What had been more general denunciations of the smothering of the beauties of nature with factories and city slums and tenements — 'the sulky blotch upon the prospect' of Dickens' Coketown — became more particular warnings of the ways in which the sustenance of the industrial population depended more and more upon forms of violence to the earth that nourished them. One of the great ironies of the anti-urban rural nostalgia among successful entrepreneurs who could not wait to turn their children into versions of country gentlemen (which Martin J. Wiener discusses in *English Culture and the Decline of the Industrial Spirit*), is that it only further concealed the real damage that was being done, not so much to the industrial spirit as to the real countryside. It is true, as Wiener says, that 'the country was to be all that modern life was not, a psychic balance and refuge'; but in the process the physical balance of nature was to be seriously disturbed. The fantasy only served to dissimulate the degradation of the earth, that was chronicled by more sober and practical farmers and countrypeople of the period.

The consequences of this, not only for Britain, but for the wider world, were by the 1930s becoming clearer. Jacks and Whyte wrote in *The Rape of the Earth,*

'Man-induced soil erosion is taking place today in almost every country inhabited by civilized man, except north-western Europe. It is a disease to which any civilization founded on the European model seems liable when it attempts to grow outside Europe. Scarcely any climate or environment is immune from erosion, but it is most virulent in the semi-arid continental grasslands — the steppes, prairies and velds of North and South America, Australia, South Africa and Russia — which offer the greatest promise as future homes of civilization. It is also the gravest danger threatening the security of the white man and the well-being of the coloured man in the tropical and sub-tropical lands of Africa and India.'

So many of the environmental crises of the last quarter century had already been foreseen and described long before, but were readily consigned to oblivion by the more pressing needs of conciliating a restless and hungry working class. John Stewart Collis, in *The Triumph of the Tree,* wrote soon after the Second World War,

'When trees were regarded by the uninstructed minds of superstitious men as the guardians of fertility, there was some sense in it. When they became simply 'timber' in the eyes of the unsuperstitious and instructed men who cut them down indiscriminately, the consequences

11

are so bad that modern science is busy restoring the idea that after all trees do guard the fertility of the soil . . . By virtue of cooling the air and spraying the sky and multiplying the clouds they exert considerable influence upon the fall and distribution of rain; by virtue of sponging the earth around their feet they enormously influence the behaviour of floods, the discipline of rivers, the supply of springs, the health of fish and (when man arrives) the welfare of navigation; and by virtue of their power to suck up moisture by the ton, they dry the swamps and control the malarian mosquitoes. Forests are so much more than meets the eye. They are fountains. They are oceans. They are pipes. They are dams. Their work ramifies through the whole economy of nature.'

In 1951, Friend Sykes in *Food, Farming and the Future* pointed out that 'all real wealth comes from the farmlands, the forests and the mines. There is no other wealth provided by nature. The only part that man performs in this scheme of things is to make use of the provision of nature in its many forms. These need to be organized and arranged equitably for the benefit of the whole community. There has never yet been created a system of economics that achieved this . . . I would call attention to the operation of nature herself. Her mineral deposits are a constant factor, but the growth of her agricultural lands and her forests is not. Here we are dealing with a living quantity. Here, we have production and we have reproduction. We are dealing with life, and life alone should be the basis of a controlled economy. Life creates life, and so long as the integrity of the cycle is maintained by the succession of birth, growth, maturity, death and decay, so that out of decay springs the resurrection of life, life can go on to the end of the world.'

The reason for the sinking into oblivion of these — once more obvious — truths is pointed out by Edward Hyams in *Soil and Civilization*, 1952.

'In the first half of the nineteenth century the rising class of machine-owning capitalists in Britain required hands to man their rapidly-growing factories. Men and women were attracted away from work on the land, or in cottage industries, where the food they ate was only what they could produce by their own actions applied immediately, or at one remove, to the soil. They were brought together in great and crowded numbers and food was brought to them in exchange for machine minding. Conditions were, in fact, created, in which they could propagate their kind, for a time and very uncomfortably, without reference to 'natural' supplies of food, to weather, to the season. The consequence was a temporary and fantastic specific (not, of course, individual) prosperity of mechanical man. Mechanical or machine-minding man became numerous out of all proportion to the supply of food within the range of action of individual machine-minding men. Among the consequences of this destruction of balance were the American dustbowl and the British Empire ... Man, over a very great part of the surface of the earth, has become a disease of soil-communities, and this catastrophe derives quite as much from his past relations with the soil, as it does from his present ones; either he has reacted from past practices, or he has failed to learn from them, or he has transferred practices which succeed in one environment, to soils where they are pernicious.'

Together with a sentimental rural nostalgia in Britain, went a reckless insensitivity towards the real natural base of the world, no doubt because we became accustomed to despoiling other people's lands for the 'raw materials' that fed industrial growth and expansion. More than this; many of the products of Empire became the meagre consolations of the industrial poor in Britain. The plantations, cash-crops and monocultures that replaced traditional sustainable farming practice abroad furnished the people

13

at home with tea, snuff, tobacco, the rice for puddings, tins of pineapples and peaches for high days and holidays, cloves for toothache and apple pies, chocolate for their children's treats, oranges for Christmas stockings. Not only did the destruction of indigenous industry and agriculture abroad open up markets for British manufactures, but the pillage of the natural products of empire also helped conciliate the mass of the people to an economic system that oppressed them. From the very beginning, it is impossible to separate environmental degradation from the ways in which human need has been articulated to those destructive forces.

It is scarcely surprising that the prophecies and warnings of those who cared about the earth should have been by-passed, and indeed, suppressed. They were overtaken by more pressing requirements — the urgent need to attach a restless and increasingly self-assertive working class to the social and economic order that had called it into such turbulent existence in the first place. This enterprise was given even greater impetus by the Russian Revolution and the establishment of socialism in the Soviet Union: in the presence of this enormity, and the overthrow of an order falsely declared by the rich to be 'natural', discussions about respect for nature appeared to be perverse and irrelevant. Following Marx's heroic disdain for 'the idiocy of rural life', the industrialization of the Soviet Union represented an even more violent assault on the natural base than had occurred in the early capitalist era. This only hardened general indifference towards the ruinous consequences of the paradox of what became a shared project between warring systems. The speech of V. Zazubrin at the First Congress of Siberian Writers in 1926 is characteristic: 'Let the fragile green breast of Siberia be dressed in the cement armour of cities, armed with the stone muzzles of factory chimneys, and girded with iron belts of railroads ... Let the taiga be burned and felled, let the steppes be trampled. Let this be and so it will be inevitably. Only in cement and iron can the fraternal union of all peoples, the iron brotherhood of all mankind be forged.'

A system single-mindedly dedicated to the creation of wealth must necessarily appear most fitted to ending poverty; and poverty, through all recorded time, is what most people have required relief from. The overwhelming power and strength of industrial society, its vast, monumental achievements, have offered a tangible hope to the poor that they would indeed one day be delivered from want and insecurity. However, even Adam Smith, in *The Wealth of Nations* in 1776 had admitted that the creation of wealth takes precedence over the welfare of human beings. 'The great object of the Political Economy of every country is to increase the riches and power of that country.' That human well-being is something more than a chance by-product of the workings of autonomous economic forces is simply a socialist heresy. The socialist response was simply that riches created by industrialism could be seized and diverted to more humane ends. The form of wealth-creation was not itself in question, any more than was the apparently secure natural base on which it depended.

After two centuries, the hope vested in the capitalist endeavour of wealth-creation as an answer to poverty has still not faltered. And yet, poverty is far from having been eliminated. The riches themselves have served as the raw material for the manufacture of strange new forms of poverty. It is clear that poverty, in one guise or another, is indispensable to the constant need for growth and expansion of the capitalist system. Poverty cannot be 'cured', for it is not a symptom of the disease of capitalism. Quite the reverse: it is evidence of its robust good health, its spur to even greater accumulation and effort.

It is the greatest of ironies that at the very moment when those suppressed and elided arguments about the fragility of the natural base that is expected to support destructive economic systems, have become far more urgent than they have ever been, more and more people on earth should have been brought into a more total and inextricable dependency upon the workings of those economic structures for their subsistence. All the objections ever raised against the unbridled development of industrialism suddenly come together in a most explosive way: the apparently limitless capacity of human beings to consume the irreplaceable treasures of the earth without ever, for all that, assuaging a gnawing and unappeasable sense of insufficiency, is a seemingly unstoppable and dynamic process that depends parasitically upon the accelerating depletion of the world's resources. In this context, poverty, far from being a response of human beings to natural scarcity, is an elaborate artefact, a human-made phenomenon, a hunger induced by the needs of an industrial system. The problem is not simply one of an 'environment' to be conserved: the natural base is being used up by ways of living that are symbiotically articulated to the wasting and perishing of its fragile fabric. Just as the poor of the earth drive the engines of global production with their muscle and sinew and labour, so the rich of the earth — and that now means a majority in the rich Western countries — fuel those same engines with their needs, desires, wants and wishes; and all are impoverished in the service of these autonomous and impersonal processes.

With the spread of a single form of development all over the world, the blighting, parasitic monoculture of money, both its beneficiaries and its victims are impoverished in one way or another, and at the same time the face of the planet is mutilated.The malign effects of industrial life upon nature, foreshadowed in Britain by the writings of agriculturalists and farmers earlier this century, now appear in aggravated and intractable ways in virtually every country in the world; and at the same time, more people than ever before are being drawn into a debilitating dependency upon the way of life thus created. In this way, the warnings against unsustainable practice become more urgent, and the consequences of not heeding them more dire. In India,

'the Green Revolution strategy sought to master and overpower nature and to 'emancipate' agriculture from its cycles. It consisted of promoting a handful of crops, and among them a handful of exotic varieties, uniformly, across altogether diverse agro-climatic zones, with a standardized regimen of farming practices. And it aimed to maximize grain (or lint or oilseed) yields alone, on an exclusive basis — i.e. at the expense of the rest of the plant, which is why dwarf varieties, which alone can bear the weight of the grain, became necessary. This it sought to do through reliance on high-energy, high-cost, industrial or laboratory-made inputs, whose use had to be specially 'extended' to the farmer.

'The damage that this strategy has done to the environment is only now beginning to be understood: steady depletion of micro-nutrients from the soil and utter disruption of its natural chemistry, lowering of the water table to new depths, sometimes as low as 100 or 200 feet, inadequate recharging of underground aquifers due to higher evaporation losses, destruction of the contours of the land leading to excessive water run-off and topsoil erosion, spread of salinity and waterlogging, and the poisoning of the air, water, land and vegetation by toxic agro-chemicals on an extensive scale. All this must be placed in the context of deforestation, misguided emphasis on large dams which disrupt whole watersheds, and unrelieved land and water mismanagement.' (Praful Bidwai, *Times of India* 20.2.88).

If it were merely a question of rescuing and applying sustainable practices, this might not present too grave a problem; but it also means dismantling the distorted relationships both between people themselves and between people and these processes of maldevelopment, which have taken on a life of their own. There are at least three levels

17

at which the evil requires to be confronted: (1) the absolute impoverishment of the poorest; (2) the growing dependency of the rich upon the maintenance of these patterns of development (itself a form of impoverishment also); and (3) the damage inflicted upon the earth by this malign dynamic.

We can read in various sites all over the world the different stages of development that we in Britain have passed through. In the early industrial period, Britain could pass on the costs of expansion to other parts of the globe, 'virgin' territories, captive peoples, unspoilt unconquered countries. There no longer exist any such convenient spaces upon which such costs can be displaced; and this is why a day of (wholly secular) judgment now confronts the planet.

This book shows — only fitfully and partially — how each successive stage of the fixed and predictable trajectory of 'development' offers the people it touches the hope of relief from poverty; a poverty which instead of being transformed into sufficiency, a modest and satisfying plenty, simply turns into another form of poverty. The constant factor is the multiple and varied ways in which humanity is wasted in this malign project, servicing as it must, impersonal processes of wealth-creation that know nothing of human things, but which impose their own inner compulsions that must be obeyed. From self-reliant tribal society, destroyed by the felling of the forests that have nurtured it for millennia, to the 'modernized' rural sector which displaces so many subsistence farmers in favour of highly mechanized and capitalized agriculture; from the people driven by hunger and landlessness from the countryside to squat in the slums and workshops of the cities in the South, to those journeys of escape from the inner cities to the sprawling suburbs and beyond; in the migrations from Third World to First World, the passage from peasant to proletarian, and from worker to petit bourgeois, there is the same promise of relief from insecurity and privation; and yet all these changes immiserate in one way or another, they always take something away from the people affected by them, whatever benefits may also appear in the process of transition.

It is a form of development that can never emancipate. It can change the form of people's subordination, it can modify the nature of the poverty they experience, but it does not liberate. Even the very richest in the world complain above all about all the things they must forego, the money they don't have, the wishes they must renounce, the commodities and experiences they cannot afford. Even the most privileged are compelled to bear within themselves the urgency for striving to acquire, the compulsion to wealth that has nothing to do with human need, but is part of a soulless system that we must inhabit and which inhabits and animates us. It is a form of possession, whereby we have come to identify our deepest human needs with the inescapable necessities of one particular economic system, so that we no longer distinguish between our own unappeasable hunger and its insatiable search for profit.

One of the most urgent tasks for an alternative, Green politics is to demystify wealth, to remove the sacred aura with which it has been invested. This cannot easily be accomplished by exhorting people to renunciation. It is no good saying 'Give up this or that benefit of industrial society'; sacrifice without reward is a thin fare for a political project as generous as that which underlies the Green movement. What we can perhaps promise is a liberation from the many sicknesses that necessarily accompany this version of riches on which we have become so dependent: the addictions, the violence, the fear and insecurity, the ravages of drugs and alcohol, the avidity for escape, the emotional and spiritual disturbance, the anxiety and stress, the cancers, diseases and disablements that have been too readily accepted as the other part of the price we pay for the material benefits. The system that has delivered the goods to so many in the rich world has also delivered some powerful evils; and these are, as it were, the forfeits imposed upon the rich for the way in which they have abused the poor of the earth and the injury inflicted upon the planet itself.

Nothing is more destructive than the corrosive power upon the richest of their wealth. Of course the rich were not always, as they have become in our time, the objects of such universal veneration and emulation. It is true, as the historian Fernand Braudel declares 'the rich are doomed to prepare the future life of the poor. It is, after all, their justification: they try out the pleasures that the masses will sooner or later grasp;' but there were, at an earlier stage of industrial development, doubts that the poor must aspire to be the mere mechanistic aspirants to ownership of what the rich possessed. William Morris was not afraid to speak of a society in which 'humanity was wasted in one way or another by penury or riches.' And earlier, Thomas Carlyle (in *Past and Present*, 1843), wrote

'In Poor and Rich, instead of noble thrift and plenty, there is idle luxury alternating with mean scarcity and inability. We have sumptuous garnitures for our Life, but have forgotten to LIVE in the middle of them. To whom, then, is this wealth of England wealth? Who is it that it blesses; makes happier, wiser, beautifuler, in any way better? Who has got hold of it, to make it fetch and carry for him, like a true servant, not like a false mock-servant; to do him any real service whatsoever? As yet no one. We have more riches than any nation ever had before; we have less good of them than any nation ever had before . . . In the midst of plethoric plenty, the people perish; with gold walls and full barns, no man feels himself safe or satisfied.'

This sceptical view of existing versions of wealth long ago became marginalized, just as the degradation of the environment became a secondary consideration in the sublime interest of the creation of such wealth. The first thing in any Green endeavour for a satisfying sufficiency for all people on earth must be to puncture the pretensions of the rich, to undermine the reverence they command in the absence of any higher source of values, to desacralize the sense of the numinous that hovers over their vast fortunes.

For what exactly is being held up for our wonder and admiration? The rich are nothing more than the most monstrous predators upon the earth's resources, the cannibalistic devourers of the substance of the poor. Are we seriously expected to applaud their prodigious appetites, their bottomless capacity for using up and spending? They are the most baleful force ever unleashed upon the world, the ransackers of its beauties, the plunderers of its natural treasures, the greedy and parasitical exhausters of its fragile covering. Their purposeless mobility, aimless heaping up of possessions, their costly pleasures and gilded palaces, their powers of consumption make of them a disease. There is no problem of poverty, or there would not be, but for the more intractable problem of wealth and its abusive and monopolistic control of the necessities of the poor. In the restless search for answers to their fathomless needs, their inexhaustible wants and ineffable desires, they seem sublimely unaware that their showy progression through time has such devastating consequences of the world. The adulation and flattery that surround them offer shelter from the consequences of their actions; they buy the simulation of approval and congratulations for their destructive passage through life, even though they are hastening us all towards the time when waste and chaos will once more cover the face of the earth. Their wealth has elevated them to the position of strange secular deities, whose cults demand the daily sacrifice of human beings all over the earth, whose appropriation of all things is directly connected with the avoidable disease and hunger and want that send so many to their graves even as they draw their first breath.

What is there in the rich that we should revere them, defer to their money? Is it that their whims can send armies of workers into the depths of the earth to fetch gold or silver for their adornment; that their caprice can cause whole forests to be felled for the sake of dessert fruits out of season that must be brought to their table; that their faintest desire can summons sweatshops full of people into existence, sewing and stitching and decorating with gold thread their briefly fashionable garments? Should we be dazzled by their capacity to manipulate unseen, distant others into doing their dirty work of violating the earth for them, so that they gain immunity from any direct involvement in these unpleasant developments? Should we not wonder at the way their human powers have all been superseded by the power of making money, and all their self-reliance, invention, creativity and ability to do things for themselves have all been overtaken by the supreme ability to buy? Should we not rather stand amazed at the emptiness within that is the consequence of the glittering spectacle without, the gutting of a humanity so that the measureless achings and absences can never be compensated by the purchased consolations?

Should we not rather pity the decay of the imagination of extreme wealth, locked as it is in those predictable and material images of its own expression of value: the ugly mansion with its electronic security, the villa overlooking the polluted sea, the display of jewels and furs, the silver Rolls-Royce, the liveried attendants, the aimless travel, the designer dresses, the public occasions, the premiere and the night-club, the casino and the marina; and with them the bought civility, the paid-for smiles, the inauthentic and simulated pantomime of respect from an employed entourage. How would they ever know real tender feelings or unfeigned concern, passed as all emotions must be through the severe filter of their wealth?

There is no more depressing experience than to wander through the gallerias and malls where the very rich express themselves through buying, and to see there the plundered imagination laid out, defunct, in the elegant displays of merchandise. I once spent half a day in the enclosed shopping area of the Taj Mahal Hotel in Bombay, which is like a metaphor for the false environment imposed by wealth upon the real environment of poverty, wretchedness and loss. The silks and the fabrics, the ivory work and animal skins, the leatherwork and embroidery, the filigree earrings and delicate metalwork, the carpets and drapes and hangings, woodwork in the most precious and scented products of the tropical forest, precious stones and gold rings and chains and amulets, the bangles of impossibly coloured glass, head-dresses and sarees, peacock-feather fans, sables and white foxes, necklaces and anklets — what a freight of materialised imagination, and what cruelty and sadness in their musky presence in these airless chambers.

Above all, the rich take great pains to cloak their conduct with money, to buy distance and discretion and present to the world an appearance of the utmost urbanity and civility. Yet their role as models and inspirers of the rest of us means that the facade of imperturbable calm, luxury and happiness can rarely be maintained for long. Their dissimulated sufferings show through, in spite of the anonymous detoxification clinics, private psychiatric care, purchased therapies and attempts to heal the debilitating sicknesses of their addiction to money. Their sorrows do surface through the newspaper scandal, the shocking court-case, the mysterious death, the golden children destroyed by drugs or killed while driving at 120 miles an hour on the wrong side of the motorway, the exotic divorce, the overdose and the discreet clinic and the island hideaway, the slashed wrists before the revelations of sophisticated peculation, electronic fraud or insider dealing. All these things must be tolerated in their martyrdom to wealth.

And it is a real martyrdom. Who can tell what falsifications and inauthenticities they must go through in their tireless service to money? Just occasionally, the extent of their sufferings can be gauged from what seeps, despite themselves, into the public domain.

During August 1987, the popular press was obsessed with stories of the transformation of the pop star Michael Jackson. They dwelt with great relish on the number of operations he had had, of just what had been involved in the process of refashioning and reshaping his face and his colour. An article in *France-Soir* recorded an interview with two leading French plastic surgeons: the operations in themselves were not remarkable; it was only the concentration of them in a single face that was extraordinary. The surgeons said

'he is a completely artificial personage; as he grows older there is every chance that he will not be able to tolerate what he has done to himself, particularly as his fame wanes. The lightening of the skin may result in blotchy depigmentation. It may be that he finds his colouring is not even, and this will have to be covered up with cosmetics. The lips and eyes shouldn't be a problem — the Japanese go in for blephoroplastics — but a local infection could leave his nose in difficulties. It appears that he has had a plastic graft. That could be dangerous; in the long run, it could leave him with a hole where his nose was. He must under no circumstances be hit in the face.'

The star is an artefact: transformations, changes of personality are the proper concerns of show business; and yet, he offers the most stunning comment on the use of medical resources in a world where so many of the injured and mutilated must drag the stumps of their abdomen on leather pads, or paddle with their diseased limbs along the roadways of the Third World cities. Jackson's metamorphoses are justified as a tool of his labour in the context of the media in which he lives.

According to the popular press, the psychiatrists say that Jackson has remained a child. He is, par excellence, the adult who is an infant. He will never grow up. It was reported that he leaves the fortress of his mansion only to go to Disneyland, and the place has to be opened up specially for him, because he will not go when other people are there. He adores video games, and is reputed to sleep in an oxygen chamber.

At the same time, he is the idol of millions of young people, one of the most highly remunerated stars in the world. What is it about him that his votaries admire? The looks that have been created by plastic surgery, the personality that is a figment, the image that is pure fabrication? That a whole generation of children are being raised in the presence of such models of insubstantiality and fantasy would be bad enough; but it is only the image on their bedroom walls that they see, and the ghostly voice they hear. The rich themselves are abused and exploited in the process; but at the same time vast quantities of 'wealth' are created in this disordered world of surfaces and false appearances. Should we wonder if violence, disturbance and confusion are some of the by-products of these aberrations? The ultimate achievement of an enterprise culture increasingly disarticulated from human need is synthetic human beings, phantoms before which real flesh and blood is expected to bow down.

The multitude of poverties generated by such forms of wealth can never be remedied by an intensification of them. The further effects of these may be seen in the used-up necessities of the poor, the inner desolation of the rich and in a blighted planet. This book is concerned with the way in which the race for riches bypasses more modest and realizable goals of sufficiency and a modest plenty; and leads only to mutations of poverty: to loss, dependency, insecurity — a condition that can be cured only by liberation into a sustainable equilibrium with the earth that must bear us all.

CHAPTER TWO

The inner city

Introduction

The decay of much primary industrial activity in Britain over recent years has been represented as a release of the people from dirty and dangerous manufacture — an unqualified blessing. Yet at the same time, this profound restructuring of the economy has also withdrawn from many people control over the materials with which demonstrably useful and vital things were made; it has prised from their grasp that 'sensuous reality' that was formerly a source of their potential power and a focus for struggle. In a world where so many objects of daily use are manufactured in the four corners of the earth, the former industrial workers have no role, no significant contribution to make. The sense of impoverishment and loss that this creates underlies much of the malaise in the old industrial areas, at the heart of the former manufacturing towns and cities.

The inner city

The nature of poverty in the rich world can perhaps be best understood by looking at what has come to be called the inner city, and the people who live there; for their lives bear the scars of the violence that has been done to human beings in the sublime mission of preserving a sense of insufficiency at the heart of the richest societies in the world.

The inner city is a deeply ambiguous term. First of all, most people living in 'inner city areas' almost never use that expression about the places where they live. 'What do you mean?' they ask, 'this isn't the inner city. This is our home, this is where we live.' Or they imagine you are thinking of other places — Birmingham or Glasgow — somewhere else, not here.

There is another sense in which the inner city does not exist; for it is also just what the words suggest — an inner city — place of the imagination. After all, the New Jerusalem was also a kind of inner city, as indeed was the extraordinary semi-pastoral vision evoked by William Morris when, in the 1880s, he was describing a London of the 1950s: Hammersmith Broadway consists of 'a range of buildings and courts, low but very handsomely built and ornamented', while over them towers ' a great hall, of a splendid but exuberant style of architecture that seemed to me to embrace the best qualities of the Gothic of Northern Europe with those of the Saracenic'; while Kensington has become largely forest, and Piccadilly 'an arcade of what I should have called shops, if it had not been that, as far as I could see, the people were ignorant of the arts of buying and selling'. He also refers to 'a place called Manchester which has now disappeared'.

It is perhaps this vagueness as to what the inner city means that permits so many people who do not live there to project onto it whatever they choose. This is how it becomes both metaphor and euphemism. It is a semaphore for racists and those prejudiced against the poor. It can mean Left-wing citadels. It means concentrations of people on welfare. It means crime and vandalism. It means Trouble. In other words, the term has become a kind of dumping-ground for the toxic wastes of our hatreds and fears; pollutants that are, in many ways, even more damaging than the contaminated remains of vanished industrial processes. This cannot be emphasized too strongly; for it shows that environmental concerns are not merely a question of administrative reform, but are

27

profoundly linked to spiritual, humanitarian and ideological struggle.

What we are now seeing is indeed a form of regeneration of those places — the sites of demolished factories and derelict mills, of redbrick terraces, that dense mesh of habitations that was also a strong network of kinship, the material emplacements of human bondings and solidarities.

But for many who live in the ragged ruined places of an almost vanished industrial civilization that regeneration has meant a kind of invasion. The showplace private homes — which for their occupants represent nothing more than a rapidly appreciating asset — the corrugated metal units and warehouses in primary red and blue, the banks of saplings (why do they never grow into trees?), the 1930s-replica wine bars, contribute little to a community whose original reason for existence is now embalmed in the local museum. The developers, builders, entrepreneurs and the new rich have been busily staking their claim to what must appear to them to be virgin territory. Like so much of contemporary experience, this is all a ghostly replay of past history. For these are nothing more than colonial expeditions to newly opened-up lands ripe for conquest and the implant of alien culture; just as our forebears once penetrated to the four corners of the globe, annexing land, subduing people, changing established ways of living, converting them to new creeds — in this case, as so often before, to the emancipatory doctrines of *laissez-faire*. And just as those vanquished people were pressed into the service of the conquerors as coolies and bearers and indentured labour, so their counterparts are to be enlisted in the interests of the service economy — as daily helps, nannies, odd-job persons, and as always, servants, whether private or as employees of industrialised services.

How is it possible that this project sounds so plausible? It has to be said that in most of these areas, the Labour Party has been in power for at least 40 years, and in some, even longer. Throughout that time, there has been a sustained and often unheard complaint of the indifference, obstructiveness and deafness of those authorities to the needs of the people. In its early days, Labour worked with tireless vigour to alter what it used to call 'the environment' in which its people lived and worked. And indeed, its period of incumbency in town halls throughout the kingdom did coincide with the complete transformation of that environment on which its tired eyes have remained forever fixed — the insanitary tenements, the squalid courts and cramped back-to-backs, those workplaces so prodigal of human life and limb. In the place of these horrors the 1950s and 60s substituted the new estates and the shopping piazzas and tower blocks. (At the time, these were greeted as proof that we had indeed entered the modern age. When the first twelve-storey block of flats was first proposed in my home town, the headline in the local paper read 'Manhattan Comes to Northampton'; and who, in a dingy provincial town in the late 1950s could resist the assimilation to New York?)

Labour presided over this mutation of the inner city landscape; and mutation rather than transformation it turned out to be. So many of the old evils which the change of decor was to have abolished, reappeared slowly, stealthily through the increasingly threadbare fabric caricature of the shining city that Labour helped to construct, alas, chiefly in fantasy. Not only the same old evils, like mass unemployment and poverty, but also some that are distinctly of this age — glue-sniffing and heroin, and interesting new forms of violence and squalor. Beveridge's five giant evils, that the welfare state was to have exorcised, loom over these altered scenes, brooding, spectral, mocking. It has been a long morality play, in which Labour was destined to demonstrate its inability to eliminate barbarisms that have remained immune to reformist impulse and charitable endeavour alike. There was no dearth of Labour politicians through the whole post-war period, sitting in the foggy wastes of their cavernous city halls, declaring themselves satisfied, having accomplished what they imagined they came to power to achieve; fingering their chains of office and sitting for portraits that would take up their position in the lugubrious lengthening gallery of mayors of this borough. Even as the new buildings began to crumble, and the estates without amenity or grace became ruinous wastelands, angry Labour councillors would be interviewed on television, declaring 'We can change where people live, but we can't change people.' Beleaguered housing officers, officials and councillors — those who so rarely lived in the materialized blueprints for other people's lives — were to be seen, when cornered by a chanting crowd protesting at the building of a motorway, trying to make themselves heard above the voices of demonstrators, and finally being rescued by the police from the wrath of those they still, at least at election times, sentimentally referred to as their 'own people.'

It is, of course, easy to blame those old Labour politicians in retrospect; the vast majority acted in good faith. That they too were victims can be seen in the way in which the party that was dedicated to the removal of old abuses — rapacious landlords, exploited labour and avoidable disease — can now convincingly be represented as the *cause* of the sorrows and oppressions of the people. Those generations who have never known anything but the welfare state cannot be expected to be grateful for the abolition of wrongs they have never suffered. In any case, gratitude is thin gruel with which to nourish political endeavour. Of the compromise between capital and labour after 1945, perhaps the most memorable remark was that of the woman in Glasgow who said 'If you marry the muck-heap for the manure, you shouldn't be surprised if you get poisoned by the stink.'

The position of the inner cities cannot, of course, be separated from that of the outer estates, into which so many people were decanted (as the unlovely language of the planners describes it). The inner city is tied symbiotically to the great housing schemes — Easterhouse in

Glasgow is typical, a township the size of Perth without anything to delight the eye or please the senses in any way. The inner city is equally tethered to the vast spread of private housing, into which so many of those who could afford it bought their passage to suburbia and beyond during the same period.

The great housing estates that the Conservative government now seeks to break up are indeed places of loneliness, poverty and violence. They contain a vast reservoir of unwanted human energy, of repressed creativity which must all be channelled into getting, by hook or by crook, fair means or fraud, the money with which to live. Some of the contrivings of people must surely command the admiration of those who set such store by inventiveness and skill: the multiple identity of those doing three low-paid jobs; the woman packing her room with Jiffy-bags to muffle the sound of her machining through the night, the man moulding 50p pieces in ice to insert into the gas-meter (they melt and evaporate and leave no trace of fraud).

The process of disgracing Labour-controlled authorities has been aggravated by the Conservatives in recent years, reducing funds so that they will appear even less capable of dealing with those intractable problems that they would scarcely have been able to contain anyway. And in consequence, the Labour Party has been forfeiting its role as a vehicle of social hope, and is now seen as simply another, and not very efficient, administration.

This is what has prepared the ground for the moral rehabilitation of the values of the free markets that created so many of the evils in the first place: a humanity in bondage once more to free markets, which Labour came into the world to deliver them from. Mrs Thatcher's mission to the inner cities means that the Conservatives come in the guise of liberating army to the besieged city. When she talks of 'socialist fiefdoms' as 'the last remnants of feudalism', historical accuracy is easily submerged by the appeal to felt experience. She is going to release the people from bureaucrats, council landlords, the officials and know-alls whose business is with the leading of other people's lives. 'Anything must be better than this' says the voice of despair. That the gospel of free markets is what brought the people crowding into these sites of desolation in the first place — the hope of work in mills and docks and foundries — is concealed by the cumbrous and rusting mechanisms of improvement that have failed them. The reversal of roles is, it seems, complete.

The inner cities serve as a powerful defining edge for the majority in Britain. For while it is true that two nations have been reconstituted in our time, the poor are now the minority. While most people remained poor, all governments expressed concern for their plight, if only in the interests of dissuading them from using their numerical superiority to forcibly divest the wealthy of their treasures. But as a minority, the poor are electorally expendable; indeed, they are disfranchised as effectively as if they had never been accorded the vote in the first place.

The role of black people in these benign processes is central. The presence of black people in the industrial cities as an answer to the last brief labour shortage in the fifties and sixties in Western Europe is only a fragment of the issue. Racism in contemporary Britain, as the market economy grows more raw and naked world-wide, is not only the aftermath of an imperialist past come home to these shores. Black people are overwhelmingly among the poor in Britain. Promises were made to them (not by individuals to be sure, but written, as it were, into the iconography of progress in the culture) that their children would be the long-term beneficiaries of migration, despite all the privations they had to submit to. But those children have seen themselves even more dispossessed than their parents were, by reduced work opportunities, racism and criminalization. For black people are a reminder to the rich that the great majority of the world's people are poor and black; just as a majority within Britain were once poor. The function of black people in the rich Western countries is to demonstrate to the affluent the interest they have in preserving the existing world order. Those former migrants from the Third World and their children are the unacknowledged hostages to global patterns of power and privilege. Racism, in this context, means resentment and fear of the poor of the earth; and is the other side of all the ostentatious and charitable giving which we (literally) make such a song and dance about, but which does so little to reverse the flow of wealth in the world from poor to rich.

All this gives yet another twist to the politics of fantasy of the past decade: the yuppie invasions of the central areas of the cities are only excited and inflamed by their association with the annexation of the Indian subcontinent, parts of Africa and the Caribbean in our imperial past. We should never underestimate the power of fantasy in the rich societies of the West — the Falklands war demonstrated how readily sentiments evoked by thwarted imperial grandeur can rise up from their shallow grave to drench the present in blood.

Sites ripe for development have been discovered everywhere, and without the need for costly expeditions overseas. Great breaches have opened up in the cities; and where the people inconveniently remain, they can be easily removed. The deporting of people for the sake of the valuable land they occupy is an ancient and ignoble tradition in Britain, as indeed almost everywhere in the world. Just as in St Katharine's Dock hundreds of families were ousted for the visionary realization of the Marina in the 1970s, so in 1825, an Act of Parliament had removed more than 2000 persons for the construction of the dock in the first place. There are many examples — the people displaced from town centres over the past thirty years in the high cause of road-building, the wholesale clearances in the nineteenth century for the sake of the great railway termini. It is presently occurring all over the world — clearances took place in Seoul in preparation for the Olympics in 1988, and the largest slum in Asia (in

Bombay) has recently become the object of the attentions of developers, who can see fortunes to be made out of former marshland that half a million people have built up and improved over a period of forty years.

One of the most symbolic examples in Britain must surely be Wapping: the people who live in the shadow of the News International building see, not only the crude physical emblem of transnational wealth and power but also the outpourings of the ideology that sustains them, through *The Sun* and its more genteel relative *The Times*.

What we have seen in our era is the decay of Labour's vision of an alternative in the world, and a turning, in desperation, to the very forces that Labour was to have humanized. We can see the epic circularity of a closed system, which bred its own resistances and accorded them limited space in which to fail, the better to reappear in the world with renewed vigour and immodest triumphalism. Those inadequate responses of Labour are a warning to the new bearers of social hope in the contemporary world. Labour incorporated and then marginalized is the lesson to the developing Green movement. Those impulses, if they are to be effective, must retain their radical and liberatory impulse. It will not do to speak of administrative modifications, as though all that is required is a little adjustment at the edge of the system. We must speak a language of emancipation, the celebration of the re-emergence of social hope in a world from which it has been for so long, it seems, banished. If the Greens are to avoid the fate of the Labour Party, a more rigorous and stringent analysis of the forces opposed to them is vital; a greater imagination, a more inspiring vision to sustain them as they embark upon *their* vision of transformation. Conservationism, environmentalism are to Green politics what Labourism was to Socialism; and the consequences of that compromise are now clear. If the Green political endeavour falters, the monuments to that failure will be a wasteland infinitely less tractable to reform even than Labour's inner city dereliction; and the sombre magic of market forces will be utterly powerless to regenerate *that* blighted landscape.

Tiger Bay, Cardiff

Butetown, once the main source of labour for Cardiff's docks, is now an isolated community of 1960s development — tower blocks and streets of low-rise buildings. The reconstruction of the old docks area is taking shape all around: a new county hall, a private housing estate, and a distributor road that will link the new marina and leisure area with the centre and edge of the city.

Traces of what Butetown was like can be seen in the monumental redbrick structure of the Bute Docks Company, with its casements and gargoyles and ponderous bulk. There are the shells of a few grandiose hotels and banks, and a little of the remaining Victorian heart of the mythic Tiger Bay area. For the rest, it is mostly empty land: bollards on the crumbling quayside, yachts beached in the mud of low tide that shines like silver in the late summer sun, buddleia and willow-herb, with here and there, traces of the old patterns of little cobbled terraces and streets; places where children used to meet the sailors coming from the ships in the docks, and would charge the Americans five pounds to show them the area around the customs-house with its clubs and brothels; or they would fish in the estuary waters for whiting and mullet, clambering over the ships, and living in summer in secret hideaways, where they would catch and eat black-birds and thrushes and even grow their own potatoes.

This is the kind of area due to be developed, bringing back life to the inner city; although few of the residents of Butetown have any illusions that they will the benefici-aries. Mrs Thatcher's army of invaders are already installed in expensive houses with burglar alarms and security locks and guard dogs. 'That shows what they think of us', said one black man. 'They all have electric time-switches to turn their lights on so we won't break and enter.'

Those who have been ejected from the employment structure in the decay of the docks economy are currently being called to the Restart programme. In an old school building half a mile from Butetown, twenty people gather to listen sceptically to the advice on how to get motivated and apply for jobs. 'Counselling with menaces' was how one elderly Welshman described it. And certainly, being brought compulsorily into this public forum shows up the vulnerability of many of the people. It is a harsh exposure for the man who has to admit that he cannot read or write, and whose last job was in a factory making dolls' prams, where the metal was so sharp that his hands still bear the scars of multiple cuts; for the woman in her early fifties who registered as unemployed when her mother died after twenty years of care. This woman has still not completed the mourning process for her mother, a sad-eyed effaced person, isolated and exhausted by years of unrelieved caring, and finding there is nobody to care about her. 'They say I've had no experience; what do they think I was doing all those years' she asks bitterly. The man separated from his wife admits that he doesn't really want a job, because the maintenance payments for his five children will leave him with less than he gets on social security. One man is living apart from his wife and child because she is working: they pretend to be separated simply so that he will continue to receive benefit. 'So much for the party that's devoted to family values. It encourages you to separate. I'm not the only one — I know lots of couples doing the same thing.' A man in his twenties with two young children and another expected soon is looking after the children while his wife works. 'It's a full-time job, bringing up your children. There's no such thing as women's work any more — there's just bringing up your family. I don't want a job, but I do want it recognized that looking after a family is a full-time occupation. It always has been.' A woman of twenty-five says she survives by cooking for her brother's family and her sister's. 'For most meals there are nine of us. You learn what they call economies of scale. It also brings the family closer again. I've also learned to make my own bread, and to knit sweaters and make clothes. It's not ideal, but it has its compensations.'

Tony who is twenty-seven, says he sees the unemployed as a new monastic class. 'We're learning to do things for ourselves, giving each other as much as we can for a minimum of cash. Just as the monks in the past led a separate life, so we may be showing the world the way it will have to go to develop a way of life that can be sustained.' 'The trouble with that' comes the caustic reply, 'is that the government took the vow of poverty for us.'

There are few lessons that training programmes can teach the people of Butetown. In any case, the very presence here of so many people from different cultures is an enduring testimony to the violence inflicted by the necessities of labour on people from all over the globe: drawn from Somalia, Nigeria, the Caribbean, Eastern Europe, Scandinavia, they worked in the docks, only to see their children stranded in unemployment and poverty. Although Butetown formed a strong defensive community, it has been unable to resist those changes that will further depower them and offer them employment, if at all, only in new forms of servitude.

In Charles Street, close to the city centre, the Youth Project employs about 25 young people on community programme work. The building itself is in a conservation area: early Victorian merchants' and shipowners' houses, now far decayed. £10 000 has been spent on refurbishing the facade and painting it pastel pink, while the structure requires ten times as much to prevent it from falling down. 'It's like so many things in this society', says Ali who works at the centre, 'paint up the surface and never mind about the rot underneath.' The Youth Centre acts as a conduit through which the great reservoir of unwanted skills and powers of young people can find an expression of sorts. Ali Yassine himself was originally an apprentice airframe/engine fitter at RAF St Athan, but when his apprenticeship finished, there were not enough jobs to absorb all the apprentices who had been trained. 'We were given £1000 and that was it. We had been promised skills that would last us a lifetime. At the time it was a terrible shock, but now I'm glad. I bought a guitar with my severance money. I don't regret it now, because I play in a band — Level Vibes — and we do the backing for all the black stars who come to Cardiff.' Ali's father came to Butetown from Egypt. He studied and got a degree, but he felt that racism was so strong in Britain that he preferred to take a job with British Rail, where he would at least be with other black people, rather than work where he would get more money and be made to suffer. 'That's why I don't care about not being a fitter' Ali says. 'I made a gamble that I would play the guitar. Now we're getting known a bit, I feel it has paid off. There's a lot of talent among young people, but it doesn't get taken seriously. There's no market for it.'

Upstairs, in the carpentry class, Shirley is making a cot and a high chair for her five-month-old baby. She works meticulously, with great application. She went from Edinburgh to London looking for work. She lived in squats and lodgings and on other people's floors in Camden, and during the months she was there neglected herself so that she finished up weighing only six and a half stone. 'Cardiff was like coming to civilization. But it's impossible for young people to get anywhere to live. I had to get out of Edinburgh, drugs capital of Britain it is. But anywhere you go, as soon as you try to get a flat, when they see you're pregnant, no chance. I don't know why people are so prejudiced against children.' Shirley has finished the high chair, and is now working on the side of the cot: a highly crafted and skilled piece of work. She says 'People have got many talents, far more than are ever recognized or rewarded by this society. You should never say "I'm this or that", you can't be defined by your job, especially when so many jobs for young people are demeaning. Nobody's going to say "I'm a waiter" or "I work in a fast-food joint or a shop" and think that's the total of their identity.'

Because Butetown has been a place of close-knit and tolerant diversity, it comes as a shock to many who grew up there when they discover the depth and extent of racism in the wider society. Cyril Payne of the 3Is Centre says 'I believed that the whole world was like my mother and father. She was white and he was black, and they loved each other. I grew up thinking that's how things were. I only really woke up when I was about eighteen. That's when my education really began. I don't think you can reform the system. It is corrupt through and through, and will have to be replaced. You know why all these yuppies are coming to live down the docks area? It's because the sea is the easiest escape route for them when the people decide they've had enough and chase them all out. When I say the system is corrupt, I mean it. It breaks people. It breaks them not only by unemployment, but by drugs and drink that's just as effective a way of soaking up their energies, undermining them, keeping them down. Some of the youngsters round here use coke, that might mean £60 for a couple of sniffs, and then it's gone. They're only going to make that kind of money by hustling. What we have to do is not understand, because that is subordinate, but overstand, because that way you dominate, rise above your circumstances.'

For Cyril, Rastafarianism offers a faith of renewal and hope. 'The culture of North-East Africa predates that of Greece and Rome and Western Europe. Europe has destroyed everything it touched, and it's still destroying all other cultures. It tries to stifle black people, blanch them in its own ghost-image. Since I've identified with Rastafarianism, I feel stronger. Let my locks grow, that gives you strength, because it's natural, you're in touch with nature, with the earth from which we came and on which we depend for our life. I'm disciplined and

39

controlled. I'm a Vegan. We have to be fit and ready for the struggle, not wasting our substance on drugs and alcohol and fantasies of escape.' If Cyril Payne talks in terms of violence and revolution, this is because he is reflecting to white society the violence that he feels has been inflicted upon himself and the people of Butetown.

Tony is twenty-seven. He grew up in Butetown, but now lives with his wife and young daughter a couple of miles away. He grew up believing he was white until one day his mother left her husband, and took Tony and his brother to live in a little terraced house down by the docks. Only then did he learn that the man they had gone to live with was his father. 'And I always loved the man I thought of as my Dad; he used to take me out as a little boy to look at the stars, taught me all their names.' The man who turned out to be Tony's real father was very strict. He worked only occasionally, on the buildings, but he had a powerful singing voice, and he made a living of sorts round the clubs. 'He never earned much money, and our mother never saw any of it. He once had an audition to sing with Shirley Bassey, but for some reason he never kept the appointment. He used to sing all the songs of the fifties — Mario Lanza, David Whitfield, Dean Martin. I didn't know I had black blood in me until then. I always identified with white people. A teacher at school said to me one day "You're not like us." My heart froze when I realized what she meant. I said "What do you want me to do, act like an ape?" And I jumped on the desk and started playing up to her view of me. After that I was trouble at school. I hated it and stayed away. They sent me to a special place for truants. I left long before I was sixteen. But I loved books and reading. My father used to say to me "Don't read books, they're no use to you." I read astronomy, and I read Thucydides and Zeno and the Greek philosophers, even though I've never learnt to write very well. I've been out of work for six years. Now I don't see why I should work, I've plenty to do without paid labour. My wife works, and I've helped bring up our little girl. I'm proud of that. Surely that is enough for one person to do?'

Tony is self-taught; a sensitive and attractive man, working for the unemployed, so that they feel less isolated and impotent. He wants to unite them so they become a vital force in the world, and proclaim their usefulness outside of paid employment. 'Just because unemployment goes out of the headlines, you feel you no longer exist.'

Tony's mother still lives in Butetown, with two of his brothers. One has just applied to go into the Navy, while the youngest, a laconic, self-contained boy of 14, has constructed an elaborate pigeon-pen in the small back garden. He keeps prize pigeons for competitive racing. Birds and the sea, says Tony, were always traditional symbols of escape to the people here. As a child he used to build shelters in the waste ground, tap into the electricity supply, catch the fish that were scavenging off the barnacles on the ships by diving for them. Once, he says, they caught, cooked and ate a swan.

Tony's mother comes in from her cleaning job. She has just a few minutes before going to Bingo. She won £169 a couple of weeks ago. The pressure of the needs of the sixteen- and fourteen-year-olds give an edge to the need to win, to find money, to keep up with the things their friends have and which they feel they cannot do without. Tony remembers how he used to go round the market picking up the rotten fruit and potatoes for his mother to make a meal because there was never enough money to buy food. There is another brother who is in hospital. 'They say he's schizophrenic. Whatever it is, it comes from conflict about his identity, not knowing if he's black or white.' His mother says 'They asked me if I couldn't look after him at home. He smashed this room up, broke a glass table, put his foot through the television. He wouldn't take his tablets. I can't make him take them, I can't force him. I spoke to him on the phone today. He says he's unhappy and wants to come home. I go up there twice a week to see him. He's taken to cooking, he's going to make me a meal when I go up on Friday. But I couldn't have him here, I can't control him.' As the youngest boy goes out of the house, she calls anxiously 'Don't get into any trouble.'

In the sunshine facing the levelled ground that is to become the site of the new road, a man from Tallinn, formerly in Estonia, sits leaning on his stick. He worked in Cardiff docks for twenty-seven years after the Soviet annexation of his country. He says 'I am a country boy; sitting here, I don't see the dirty water of the bay, I can see the cornfields of my childhood. But I couldn't go back, even if I wanted to. I've no one there. I've no one here either. I've nothing to lose in the whole world. That is the freedom of the seaman.'

On the abandoned quayside, a one-storey prefabricated building houses the National Union of Seamen's office. It is staffed only by one man, Mike Jewell from Liverpool. He is melancholy and pessimistic about the future of British merchant shipping. 'They give the crewing of a ship to a Hong Kong company, they register it in Bermuda, manage it from the Isle of Man. That way, they can be free of regulations and tax. It's like any other industry, it's become footloose, mobile — shift to where you can make the quickest profit. You get a seaman coming in here, if he hasn't been paid you've got to telex Hong Kong. A lot of companies run their vessels through foreign agencies, crewed by Filipinos, some of whom have never been to sea before. P & O have always used Goan labour. In the last century, there was a volcanic eruption in Goa, and a P & O ship happened to be in the area. It rescued a lot of people. As a result, the then rulers of Goa, the Portuguese king offered P & O cheap labour in perpetuity. They can still employ Goans at £40 a week on a passenger ship. They are all doing away with British labour because it's too pricey. They'll declare a whole crew redundant on a Friday, re-hire them on Monday at cheaper wages. They'll borrow so many million pounds to do it, it'll soon be recouped employing the same people at a much lower rate. Waiters are virtually expected to live off the tips they get. Even the QE2, they sacked all the staff, then re-engaged them at a lower wage. They recruit waiters out of hotels because they don't get as much money as seamen. They blame the workers, the unions. What protection have we got against companies that span the whole world as their field of operations? It isn't less protection workers need against transnational companies; they need more.'

The people of Butetown carry an epic story of dislocation and migration, a using up of humanity, an indifference to the consequences for them and their families once they have been discarded. There is no doubt that life will come back to these inner city areas. But the poor will not go away. It is simply that they will be dispersed, no longer undiluted in whole communities. Thus they will be depowered, rendered more amenable, at least outwardly, to the civilizing truths of the market economy.

Death of a migrant

As he sank into a coma, and it was clear he would die, more and more people came to the bedside. Some were too late to say to him what they had wanted to, others remorseful that they hadn't kept in touch since they came to England, yet others talked to the inert figure, a soft monologue of remembered times. Little by little, in the cold spring days, while family slept in shifts on improvised beds and chairs, the story of his life filled itself out. Born in Grenada 47 years ago, his mother died when he was six. He had been taken to Trinidad to live with his grown-up sister and her family. There he was treated as a drudge: while his brother-in-law sat in his new taxi, and his nieces and nephews went to school, he was working the land, feeding pigs or cutting cane. The journey to England was just another stage of that early orphaning and exile. And what a long voyage it seemed now, to have travelled so far to work as page-boy in a West-End hotel, then in a plastics factory, and to die of leukaemia in a hospital bed dedicated to the memory of a president of the Wines and Spirits trade in the 1940s.

In the last few days and nights, people who hadn't seen each other for ten, fifteen years, came and went, scattered by migration, by chance, above all by the necessities of work. Someone remembers him in the hotel uniform, what an attractive figure he had been with his slim waist and long eyelashes. Visitors arrive late into the night, as they come off shift from cleaning in offices and hospitals, or straight from work in the early morning, having caught the first bus to Moorgate at 5.30am; the young people on YTS or without work; the daughter in the factory making theatrical shoes, and the youngest daughter working as a domestic in the hospital where her father is dying. I have an image of this young woman on the morning her father died. She is on her hands and knees in the stone corridor, with two older white women standing over her. She is sorting through the contents of a black rubbish sack. In the anxiety of that last day, she has lost some keys. They cannot be found; so the locks on all the doors have to be changed.

When he arrived in Southampton in 1960, he looked at the big houses with their smoking chimneys and thought they were factories. He went to live with his brother in Bedford. On the first morning, he was left alone in the flat. He didn't know how to turn on the gas-taps, and sat shivering with cold until his brother came home from work. He always told these stories with that kind of indulgence migrants have towards their own innocence when they first arrived, as though referring to another childhood, an apprenticeship to the society which was to bring such disillusion. He had not been happy with his brother. He disliked the way he treated his wife. There was a quarrel. The brother and his wife returned to Grenada long ago; but their children are at the bedside, regretting the break and the long silence between them.

I had known him for seventeen years. I learned much from him about the violence of those migrations of hope from the Caribbean to Britain; and also about the movement of people within Britain in the early 19th century, when country people had to be re-shaped for industrial society. It was the same process which drew people, 150 years later, from half way across the world, to answer a brief need for their soon expendable labour. You could feel in him what a cruel, coercive experience it was, as the human substance was being re-formed for other purposes. He had always resisted, retaining the strong moral values and the vivid imagery of his country upbringing. Of the migration that had dispersed the family, he said 'It not the day the leaf fall from the tree it go rotten.' After Mrs Thatcher's electoral triumph of 1983, he said 'Man appoint, but God can disappoint.'

He always idealized his wife. To her he brought the orphaned tenderness of his early years. Tenacious and loyal, it never wavered, even though it was abused. During the separation and divorce, the mother had won the children to her side. But that is forgotten as they sit by his bed, holding his hand, talking to him, rubbing cocoa oil into the dry dark flesh, wiping the corner of his mouth with a tissue, listening anxiously to the changing tempo of his breath.

His devotion to his wife continued even after the breakup. From the little flat in Hackney, he still followed her; this time to the Pentecostal church, where he was baptised by total immersion only six months before he died, and in spite of having been raised a Catholic. He remained ironic about the church into which he had been received, wondering why pastor's sermons dwelt at such length on the cost of telephone bills and car repairs. Why, he wondered, was there so much hatred between Christians: if we are all trying to get to the same place, the strife and jealousy must be about the place we occupy in this life.

Three weeks before his death, he dream-saw his mother. She was sewing a white cloth, patiently, laboriously. When she had finished, she tore it into three pieces, and handed them to him: one for each week he was to live. He frequently saw the distant and the long-dead in dreams. Never having had the money to go back to see those he loved, he had to fetch them to him in dreams.

Racism in Britain came to him as a shock. Once, picked up and insulted by the police, he lodged a complaint, and actually received an apology. Later, when suffering a blockage of the urinary tract, they had cut a vein in the hospital that rendered him impotent. The idea that this had been a form of enforced sterility because he was black was never far from his thoughts; although the hospital made many attempts to reverse the error by inserting a plastic splint into the penis. It never really worked.

The children wanted to send for a Catholic priest. The ex-wife said no. Pastor came; looked at him and went away. Angered by this seeming indifference, they sent for a priest anyway, who said the last rites in the early hours two days before he died. His children had vowed to be with him at the end. In the event, they weren't. They had gone home for a shower and some clean clothes. The wife alone was there.

He had been on invalidity benefit because of a heart condition. Burial on the social security meant a common grave. His daughter said 'He always had people on top of him, crowding him while he was alive; he's not having that now he's dead.' The cheapest private funeral with numbered plot would cost £825 — twice the amount that could be expected for the cheapest burial. They would find the money somehow.

The night he died, everyone came to the hospital. He looked serene and youthful. 'People the same in death as in life', said one woman; and his death was accepting and easy. The children had never seen death before: it did not frighten them. Before the body was taken to the chapel, the sister warned the family that it would have to be wheeled past where they were sitting in a metal box. Perhaps they would prefer not to see this. This had to be done, she explained, so as not to upset the other people in the ward. The tin box clattered down the stone corridor, a blue cloth draped across it, with a pillow on top, so that it looked like a stretcher.

We are allowed to see him as soon as he has been laid out in the chapel; a small underground chamber, with flowers and a large Bible on a lectern, open at Psalm 135. Everyone kisses him, and stands in a long silence. The sound of the spring rain on the windows. 'He looks like he's breathing.' 'I swear I saw him move.' 'I wonder where he is now.' 'Wherever it is, it's got to be better than here.'

Somebody has gone to fetch the other relatives. In the meantime, we wait in the hospital again. When they arrive, the chapel has been locked. Standing in the rain, under umbrellas and raincoats, waiting for a last glimpse of him. Everyone is very patient and accepting; a frieze of silent expectation, the long wait of the poor, taking for granted that this is their lot in death as in life.

The funeral takes place in a Catholic church in Hackney. The children insisted that the coffin remain open during the service. The elderly Polish priest does not articulate his words very clearly. Most of us are at a loss as to the correct responses. There is a touching moment when the priest tells of his first encounter with death: like the dead man, he was six, and his mother died.

The body looks remote now, in his best suit, hands clasped with a white handkerchief between the fingers. They have chosen their father's favourite hymns — 'Amazing Grace', 'The Lord is My Shepherd' and 'Abide with Me'. The walls of the church are painted with vivid murals, although the leaded lights of the windows are broken and patched with wood. Out on the shabby Victorian street, two old women stand under an umbrella; they cross themselves as the cortege leaves for the cemetery.

The cemetery is flooded. The grave is a narrow cavity lined with sodden simulated grass, among spreading mud-coloured puddles. The oldest daughter falls to her knees in the mud and sobs. The others hold her, take her back to the limousine. The people throw a handful of soil onto the coffin. There is a feeling of something incomplete, as though we haven't participated properly in the leavetaking. The wife looks grim: if this is a Catholic burial, her face says, then give me the Church of God. Some of the people break into a last song 'We Loved you Much but Jesus Loves You More', and join hands, splashing the earth-coloured water.

At the flat, an aunt has been cooking pots of lamb curry and rice. She has brought some home-made wine; there are also bottles of vodka, whisky, rum and Coke. The story of his life is repeated. His second daughter discovered she was pregnant the day before he lost consciousness; he would never know. They talk of the hardships they have endured — the woman brought to England by her husband with three small children. When she got here, she was expected to provide for them, and to live with them in one small room, while her man lived apart with another woman. But they submitted to all the humiliations, in the expectation that they would see their children make their way in the world; even though many of these have been even more impoverished and dispossessed than their parents were. 'We at least had each other.'

When it came to parting, everybody hugged one another and promised not to lose contact again. It all seemed such an obvious lesson: we must unite in the presence of what will be the fate of all of us. It is our anger against death and separation — those outrages against which we are powerless — that makes us turn our anger on other human beings, those upon whom that anger can have some effect, even though they are the same flesh and bone, differentiated from us only by a nuance of skin, another idiom, the colour of an eye. There flickers for a moment a bright flame of solidarity, the legacy of a penniless migrant, a brief but deep intuition that we have no enemy but death and loss.

The next generation

The migrant's grandchild was born late in 1987, and within three weeks, his son's wife also gave birth. The two beautiful children were called Belaire and Whitney. Pretty names; but the first was inspired by a shop-front in Holloway, the name of a hairdressing salon; the other by a pop singer.

Carmel, Whitney's mother, is living at home with her younger sister and the child's grandmother. She is grateful for the expertise of the older woman in looking after the baby. Grandmother holds and bathes the child with great confidence, while the mother looks on, admiring the skills of the woman with whom she has so often been in dispute, and from whose influence she has tried unsuccessfully to be free. Carmel was working in a factory making theatrical shoes. There, she met and had a brief relationship with a Welshman, some ten years older. While she was pregnant, he came to see her, said he loved her, he would do anything for her, but he wasn't free. Carmel listened sceptically to his protestations which, to her, sounded like excuses. She refused to ask anything of him, She would rather be self-reliant, although that in fact means being more dependent on her mother. In any case, he is married, and his wife was expecting a baby at almost exactly the same time as Carmel. Nor was that all. It was rumoured that the daughter of the house where he was lodging was also pregnant. Carmel said cynically 'You think you're special, and you turn out to be one of a crowd.' He is an unhappy and anguished man. His parents separated when he was a child, and he went to live with his grandmother. She died suddenly when he was eleven, and he felt he had been orphaned a second time. This left him with a great insecurity, and what seems like a compulsion, according to Carmel, to leave orphaned children all over North London. The baby looks like him, which makes it the harder for Carmel to bear; the baby's skin is pale, she has blue eyes. Carmel felt hurt that he made no effort to see the child, and didn't even call until she was three months old.

There are enough members of the family around for Whitney to be provided with everything she needs. To be raised on welfare, as seems likely to be her fate, is not as disagreeable as it may sound. It isn't the child who suffers, but the mother, who is not happy with the full-time role. She is, she says, fed up. Not bored, she insists, because that would be insulting Whitney. But she lacks the stimulus of work. She has become very thin since the little girl was born. She is very elegant, dresses very smartly, would like to be a model. 'My child is going to have the best there is', she asserts fiercely. 'She'll get a better education than I had, she'll have all the advantages I didn't.' The grandmother sniffs. That is precisely what she had said about her children. The grandmother gets up at half-past four in the morning to go cleaning. She regularly has to wait up to half an hour for a bus in the cold winter mornings, but all her earnings are now lavished on the baby. She is giving less of her money to the church, and is less keen on going on the week-long missions to distant parts of London.

The room of the council flat is cluttered. There is a painting of the Last Supper, a modern picture of a naked male and female up to their waist in water in a tropical setting; an amateur painting of the house in Jamaica where the grandmother grew up, with its verandah and plantain and banana trees all around. There are pictures of the old people, faded and smiling. Everywhere there are baby clothes and cots and toys and blankets, and photographs of the child, the first taken at birth. It seems that even in her brief life, they have spent a great deal of time making a record of her growth. She has everything that she could possibly want — the most elaborately made and fashionable clothes, a whole menagerie of soft toys. No previous generation of children have ever been the inheritors in advance of so many material things, even in this family, which is far from rich.

The sense of expenditure on the child as a stringent duty exists almost independently of what she actually needs. It seems one of the saddest aspects of this culture, that what parents do out of love — and out of pride ('No child of mine would ever wear anything second-hand' says Carmel) actually creates in the child a deep dependency on buying and the money-culture. It is very difficult for those whose story has been one of ageless and continuing poverty to accept that the heaping up of material things and the procuring the money to go on doing so is not necessarily a liberating influence upon the child, but rather stultifies and inhibits. Money becomes the sole enabling agent. Yet with the family's memories of things that are improvised, home-made, makeshift, of belongings that were functional and inexpert, the barest necessities, the purchased plenitude looks like freedom. It is actually a way of transferring people from one form of poverty — insufficiency, natural scarcity — into another, in which the imagination, ability and creativity remain dormant, the curiosity unawakened, because the only access to joy, excitement, experience and transcendence is through the straitening and narrow conduit of money.

So it is also with Belaire. Wayne, Carmel's brother, lives with Karen. Karen already has a boy of seven, a lively and attractive child. They live on an estate built in the 1970s, hard concrete surfaces, cold and hostile. The relationship between Karen and Wayne is uneasy. Since the baby was born, they have had many violent arguments. Karen called the police and said that Wayne had hit her and threatened the baby. He was arrested and kept in the cells overnight, and the magistrates fined him £150 for threatening behaviour. He resents wasting money that he could have spent on Belaire. Wayne, in spite of his dreadlocks and intense eyes, is a gentle young man, and his daughter is a source of constant astonishment and delight. Karen is proud that the health visitor said she wouldn't need to come very often, because it is clear that Karen doesn't lack confidence and knows what she is doing. Karen is herself one of eight children, so Belaire is inundated with presents. Indeed, she already has everything: a big blue panda and yellow tiger, clothes and shawls of the most delicate lace, more bonnets and bootees than she can possibly ever wear. They have a baby book, in which to record her weight and growth. It also has space to list all her relatives, all the visitors she has had and the gifts they brought. It invites the parents to make a note of the most popular film and song and book of the year in which she was born. On front of the album there is a picture of a very rosy, very white child. The flat is well-furnished and up-to-date. Wayne is watching American football on TV. The only icon in the room is a picture of Bob Marley. Wayne says he wants his little girl to grow up free and happy, but he worries whether she will be allowed to. Wayne says he can't use the pubs round here. 'There's three, and I've been into all of them. You don't see a black face. There are several National Front families on this estate. I have to go to Hackney if I want to drink. I always say hello to people. If they won't have anything to do with you, well that's up to them. You can't make people be friendly. But I wonder what kind of a world she will be growing up into.'

The most persistent response to these children born in 1987 is that they are going to be spoilt; an ambiguity of which those who express it are not always aware. Of Whitney, her aunt says 'I call her princess.' 'Everybody runs round her.' 'She's gonna have whatever she wants.' 'She rules this house.' The young child has always been the repository of dreams and hopes and longings of parents and older people; yet the culture of self-conscious spoiling is a real one, and it means precisely what it says. It invites children to instant enjoyment, of the child getting what it wants immediately. There is no question of delayed gratification or deferred pleasures or earned sweetnesses. The wants of children have become sacralized. It is a sort of aristocratic mass culture, and it feeds them into a model of imperious demands, where whim, caprice, longing and the profoundest needs become indistinguishable. It can be very spoiling indeed, where parents believe it is their highest duty to respond to all those wants of children which the society implants and fosters with such sedulous care. Many children swiftly learn what they want, and then never learn anything else. It is a strange twist of the established order that the rich and privileged now buy for their children discipline and frugality and self-restraint. Private education, for instance, involves the learning of containment and delay in answering wants. What was once imposed upon the poor for the purposes of industrial discipline is now an increasingly rare and sought-after luxury. For most children, their experience is of spending every penny as soon as it is in their hand, of giving themselves over to all the consolations and compensations that can be bought for so many obscure absences in their lives — especially those of function and of social purpose and hope. Living in the present is the dominant value of this culture; but the privileged know that if they are to survive that culture they must look to the long-term protection of their wealth and power. The spoiling of children means that they will always be instantly separated from their money; that they will have few controls and little self-discipline, which will render them constantly manageable, manipulable by their superiors. This creates a far more pliant human being than those brought up to the old rigidities of repressive and coercive discipline. Those rigidities, those values of self-denial are now the refinements of the rich alone, who temper their indulgence with one eye firmly on the future; while the poor live as though there were no tomorrow. This is an inadequately explored reversal of roles. It keeps the poor as effectively subordinate; and in that way, the forces of conservatism wear another appearance from that which was traditional. That our children require to be liberated from *the caricature of liberation* in which they live makes it all the harder for those who desperately want their children to have the best in life: what that best might be is as effectively concealed from them as it always has been.

Old in a cold season

The streets behind the town centre are bleak and deserted in the days at the turn of the year, between the paroxysm of spending at Christmas and the January sales; skeletons of Christmas trees, soiled wrappings and torn crackers overflow the dustbins, and the cats run away down the alleys with the remains of the chicken carcase. It is easy to forget that the inner city also means the old; those mute and unconsulted witnesses of change whose comment is so rarely invited.

Here are the heroic and self-effacing daughters who remain with elderly parents, starting up in the night at the sound of the old calling the long dead in their sleep; here is the untold nightmare of those who, exhausted themselves, see their retirement as a time of attending the needs of the frail and infirm. Daisy, in her sixties, with her mother of ninety-two, can never leave her for more than the half-hour it takes to do the daily shopping. Her ritual has scarcely varied for twenty years: waking at 5.30am, the cup of morning tea, getting the old woman onto the commode, warming the milk for a handful of cornflakes; dressing her, pulling the puckered stockings over the tiny feet, plaiting the hair, reminding herself to prepare the brussels sprouts, to administer the physic and the tablets at the right time, to make sure that the meal is ready by 11.45am — an egg and some mashed potato; then the washing up, the faint smell of greens permeating the afternoon, the silence of the after-dinner sleep. Daisy can never relax with the tension of knowing that her mother may die at any moment, the fear of knowing that she will never — could never — have done enough. She speaks with feeling of the lonely hours, the gesture of kindness from a stranger that makes the tears flow so easily. It would be unthinkable for Daisy not to look after her mother. Forty years ago, she herself had anorexia, 'as they call it now', she says grimly. At that time, there was no name for what she suffered. 'Mother looked after me

then. It went on for years, I was in and out of the psychiatric hospital — they didn't call it that then either. The
people in the street used to gossip, they weren't sympath-
etic. My Dad wanted to paste a copy of the doctor's report
in the window, but Mum said no. While they're gossiping
about Daisy, they're not pulling anyone else to pieces.
Mother gave me those years, it's only right I should return
them now.'

Framed against the late afternoon light, the old woman's
face is dark. Her breathing is painful, the words come
hoarse and slow. She has seen the decay of the welfare
services in the years when she has most needed them. 'It
makes me ashamed to be English', she says, of the burden
that has fallen so completely on her daughter. The words
of her dying days are curses against the cruelty of this
government. 'She still has her faculties', says Daisy. 'Of
course, she forgets what day it is. She'll say 'Why haven't
we had the football results? 'Not on a Tuesday Mum', or
'Are we going to watch Songs of Praise?' 'It's not on on
Friday.'

By late afternoon, the pyjamas are warming on the gas
fire, the slice of bread and butter and the warm milk are
ready, the hot water bottle is in the bed in the parlour.
Then Daisy sits down with the paper, but her attention
easily strays. She sleeps on a makeshift bed in the living
room so that she will hear if her mother calls. 'You never
sleep, not the deep sleep you need. Your ears are always
straining.' The low wattage bulb burns orange through
the frosted glass of the front door; the waxed dado is
burnished by its light. Daisy says 'You have a duty to
them; and anyway, I love her.'

The sisters in their mid-eighties have lived together
longer than either was married to her husband: the one
divorced after twenty-two years, the other widowed after
twenty-five years nursing her husband who got TB in the
Navy, the year he was off Archangel taking on the refugees
from the Bolshevik revolution. Their thirty-eight years
together have grown into a companionable dependency,

half-resented, half of the deepest affection; the one sharp-eyed but physically immobile, the other deaf and sweet-natured. The house they refuse to give up is full of traps and dangers: thick woollen cuffs hover over the gas-ring, the loops of frayed mats and rugs, the stairs steep and sharply angled; and there is fear now of the familiar neighbourhood, where once they knew everybody. They remain in a sort of competitive longevity, surviving somehow by the long years of habit, by reducing their needs — never great in their stoical generation. Women who left school at fourteen to work in factories, re-reading Dickens over Christmas, and recalling childhoods of a different kind of poverty from that of their old age, with its depleted company, its sparse and perfunctory visits. 'I was so ashamed of where we lived, I gave a false address at school. The headmistress called me to her study. "This isn't where you live, is it?" "No Miss Parnell." "You must always give your correct address my dear." There were tears in her eyes.' They recall the underground kitchen where they lived, and the night when the woman next door was murdered. 'The bloke she was going with had lost his wife, he'd been left with a houseful of kids. He thought Rose was going to marry him and mother his children. When he found out she had a husband already, he strangled her.' Her sister takes up the shared memory. 'One Christmas Eve, a woman rapped on our door. She said to Mother "Your old man's laying dead drunk in the middle of the road with a rabbit in his hand." She rushed out, because that was our Christmas dinner, for twelve of us. He was there, but by then the rabbit had gone. She said she wished it had been the other way round.'

What do they think of, in the short days and long nights, those who need so little sleep? Sam, seventy-nine, remembers cycling as a youngster to the Crematorium with the body of his still-born brother in a shoe-box. Sam has been a labourer all his life, living in lodgings. He spent 30 years in the same place, without a day's illness, never defaulting on the rent. When he became ill with cancer, the landlady told him to get out. 'I don't want to be phoning the doctor for you at all hours.' Sam is not bitter. 'She'd not long lost her son in a motor-bike accident. Why should she want to be bothered with me?'

Florence, eighty-two, has Alzheimer's disease. For her, it is as though the years had peeled away, leaving the most raw feelings exposed. She moved into her privately-rented flat in the most select part of town thirty-five years ago, so that she could keep up socially with her brother, then a Conservative councillor. At that time, it was a good address, the flat spacious with its stained glass, stone pillars and tympanum with Stoneleigh in gilt letters. Now seedy and overgrown, the windowpanes dusty, the ground floor is unoccupied. All around estate agents' signs are offering sound investments and luxury conversions. 'Christmas Eve? Tomorrow?' she keeps asking. 'It doesn't seem five minutes since last Christmas.' Florence sleeps in a vast dim bedroom, where the breath condenses and the mildew spreads; a photograph of her son as a choirboy, taken forty years ago, is stuck in the blemished glass of the dressing table. There is no hot water in the bathroom, the Ascot heater is rusting and disconnected. The lino is worn out and the stair carpet dingy. For years Florence kept the whole house clean, scrubbing the tiles in the hall polishing the gilt wicker table in the entrance. Now, the rent is collected by agents, more impersonal and less embarrassing to the owners who want her out in order to sell the property. Florence is thin and wasted, forgetting to eat, but remembering just enough to cover her forgetfulness. Wary and watchful, she echoes what is said to her. 'Of course', she says, 'I was always rather a cheeky girl when I was young. Your mother's family were much more staid.' She calls upon a distant coquettishness to conceal the lapses of memory, smoothing the pleats in her skirt, re-arranging the chiffon scarf at her throat. She always prided herself on living for the moment, a bold and futuristic hedonism at that time in this dour hard-working town; but she is stranded now in this derelict place, deserted by friends now that she can no longer afford the little extravagances that she once so generously offered. Of her, my mother's family would say 'She buys tulips in January', with an intonation that stated clearly what they thought of such improvidence.

In a run-down short-life house lives Phoebe, in her late seventies. There are bare boards in the living room, a hearthrug in front of the gasfire; newspaper on the table, a tin plate of minced beef for the cat. Phoebe lived with her mother until she died six years ago. 'My mother was hard-boiled. I waited on her. Every Saturday night, she sat like a queen on her throne. I had to go and get winkles for her. Fetch the vinegar. Where's the pepper. You've forgotten the salt. She used to suck the winkles and throw the shells on the fire. Then she would open a tin of Nestle's milk, drink it out, run her finger round till it was gone. On the day her own mother died, she pretended not to know, so that she wouldn't miss the outing to Leicester races. Her friends warned her that she'd dream about her. "The only thing I ever dream about is what's going to win the two-thirty at Epsom." I dream about her every single night.'

Phoebe is an intelligent woman whose abilities remained crushed, partly because of her dominating mother, but partly because she was a victim of sexual abuse as a child. 'I used to go for long walks when I was a girl. One day, I was sitting down the meadow, and this bloke walked past. He came back and took me into a field and did what he wanted to. I don't know who he was. He never spoke a word. But it upset me so, it spoiled me. I never told a soul. I was afraid people would know, by the way I walked. It's always made me tongue-tied and afraid of people. I was fourteen then.' Phoebe's whole life has been shadowed by those few minutes in 1923. Recently, her home help came one morning and, finding her still in her grubby night-gown, called her a disgrace. This was a word Phoebe always used to herself. Agitated, she threw on her best dress, combed her hair, ran out into the street. 'I'm not a disgrace now', she cried, 'I'm not a disgrace.'

Phoebe has seen her mother since she died. One day she came from the kitchen through the living-room door. 'I said to her "Hello mother." She didn't speak to me. She never even looked at me. She went straight to the table to read the racing paper. Hard-bitten in death as in life.' So many of the elderly are aware of the presence of their dead, perhaps because of the intensity with which the dead impressed them while they were alive, perhaps because of the depopulation of elderly people's lives. 'I saw my mother after she died. She was sitting on that sofa. Her face was so serene, I knew it was all right where she was. After that, I never mourned her.'

Bob, a signalman in his forties, also looking after his disabled mother, tells how, driving home from work one night, he saw a figure pass in front of the car. He got out to look. No one. He could have sworn it was his dead father. He got back in the car, drove slowly down the hill. At the bottom, there was an upturned lorry. If he hadn't stopped, he would have driven into it and almost certainly have been killed. 'I reckon I owe him my life.'

The loneliness of being old, of seeing your contemporaries die before you, has been exacerbated by the diminishing welfare services of the 1980s. One old woman said 'Thatcher told us we had to wait for the economy to pick up before we could have all the things she wanted — more hospitals, better care. Now they tell us the economy has never been better, and all we see is closed wards and cuts in services.'

More than any other group, the old have observed the changes in a society that has (once more) subordinated the most vital and precious things of life to the sacred necessities of money. As they lie awake at night listening to the gate shifting on its rusty hinge and the windows rattling in the gale, it must be for them like the recurrence of a childhood nightmare of poverty, insecurity and fear, an estrangement, amid the wealth and rapacity, from our own humanity. Their deeper, sadder wisdom has been overlaid by a kind of existential alienation, the result of the triumphal and loveless reign of those who have now held power in Britain for a decade.

Homeless men

The shift from manufacturing to service industries sounds easy and benign. But for those ejected brusquely from a tradition of heavy manual labour, it is experienced as violence. The effects can be seen in those men who occupy the diminishing number of hostel beds, who live in seedy lodgings and shared rooms, who sleep under the bridges and in derelict houses, or, if they are younger, on other people's floors.

Many casualties of these mutations in the division of labour have finished up in Brighton, a town whose prosperity and glitter goes little deeper than the peeling stucco of its Regency elegance. As one bitter veteran of its decaying bed-and-breakfast hotels said 'You want to try living in them, share a room with other people's fleas and cheesy feet and stinking breath. I'd knock 'em all down and start again.'

The day centre for homeless people, First Base, is the shell of St Stephen's church: a vast hall of fluted Corinthian pillars, ornate mouldings and an arched roof. Industrial heaters keep it warm. There are dusty chairs (rejects from defunct public transport buses) around the walls, and metal tables with formica tops. In one corner is a kitchen area, where vats of brussels sprouts and potatoes, and ovens heating thick-crusted meat pies provide a meal for 75p. On a raised platform there is a permanent sale of second-hand suits, coats of antique cut slightly discoloured with age. There are tables for pool and table-tennis and an area set aside for handicrafts.

Larry is 50: deep blue eyes, a greying ginger beard and knitted woollen hat; orange workman's oilskin, open sandals. He was brought up in a Catholic orphanage in

Brentwood, and never knew his family. 'I must have a mother somewhere', he says, 'only they wouldn't let us know who our parents were.' He was treated severely: the top joints of his little fingers are stiff and swollen. 'Your hands were always cold, and when you were caned, the fingers broke easily and didn't set.' At sixteen, he was sent to work in a bakery, greasing tins. 'I got £2 10s a week. I had to pay £2 a week lodgings, and ten shillings in bus fares. That's why I started dipping into people's pockets at work. I was said to be in need of care and protection, so they sent me to a farm for two years. Five shillings a week. Then I went in the army. I was a hopeless soldier, but I didn't want to leave. I went before the brass. 'Why do you want to sign on?' I said, 'Three meals a day, comfortable bed, good mates, something I've never had. They couldn't get rid of me quick enough.'

Larry worked on building sites, road works, labouring all over Southern England. One night, hitching a lift to his lodgings, he was asked if he wanted work.' I said Why not? So that night, pitch dark, lorry without lights, we went into this yard; kick the Alsatian in the teeth to keep it quiet, then loading this metal onto a lorry. A thousand quids' worth of stuff. I moved in with him. He lived on a council estate near Luton, had eleven kids. I stayed seven years, working with him, mainly doing safes from factories, offices, cinemas. He had a beautiful daughter of 18. She used to sit on my lap. I thought she might really like me. But that was just part of his way of keeping me there. He had no intention of letting me marry her. I couldn't leave anyway — he threatened to grass me up if I did. He had me where he wanted me.'

We got so skilled, we could break into Fort Knox if we had to; nick the safe. Sometimes we struck rich. One night, we sat in his front room, trying, to open a safe with a power drill we'd taken. A knock comes on the door. His missis opens it, and we hear the words 'Good evening officer.' Quick as a flash, my mate sits down on this safe, puts a cushion on it, grabs the baby and starts changing its nappy. I stood there rigid; I could see the brass handle of this safe sticking out. The police had been called by the neighbours — the drill was interfering with their TV reception in the middle of Coronation Street. Another time, we'd just cracked open a strong box and were sorting out the contents, when a bloody axe-blade comes through the door. The kids had been smoking in the garden shed and set it on fire. Somebody had phoned the fire brigade: they rushed through the house unrolling this hose. A few minutes later, a man with a camera and tripod arrives, starts taking pictures of us still with this strong-box on the floor. Next day, our photo is in the local paper, headline is 'Heroes save Pet Rabbits from Blaze.'

'We were supposed to be unemployed. You had to be careful not to overspend: everybody knew your dole money ran out by Tuesday, so if you flashed a tenner around or posh ciggies, they'd know it wasn't above board. Whenever we did a big job — a few hundred — the only thing was to take off in his van, go to Scotland, cool off for a while. They were good times, the hills. I could've stayed there for ever.'

Larry says he had never meant to thieve; he didn't even want to. It was a question of surviving. He has never had a home, but has always lived in the space provided by other people or institutions. 'I'm one of life's lodgers.'

'The biggest amount I ever got was 3000. The bloke I lived with was owed some money, and he couldn't get it. The guy lived in a house like a fortress. One night, I noticed the bedroom window was open just a fraction. We got the equipment — you have to be careful on council estates, everybody knows what goes on. If you're seen late at night carrying a ladder or a crowbar, that's it. Anyway, balaclava over my head, up the drainpipe, lift the window and I'm inside. I knew exactly where the box was with the money. When you break into somebody's house, they always wake up — it's a sixth sense. You have to take advantage of the element of surprise. I jumped across his bed. He let out a yell. I knew he had a son who was a strong lad, so I chucked this wooden wedge under the door, got the box and jumped back while he was still struggling to get up. I heard the son throw himself at the door. He burst in just as I was getting through the window. He grabs hold of my collar; I jump and half my clothes come away in his hands. I just run with the box, and go and lie flat in a field; that way, nobody can see you. In the box there was £3000. In the paper next day, the report said £200 stolen. What it didn't say was that the box was full of forged passports and car licences.

'I did five years in Albany, Isle of Wight. You can't fight the system, they can break you. Literally. I've seen blokes who've tried to resist, next day they're bandaged up like a mummy. They can put you in solitary, look at the walls and talk to yourself, or they'll put you in a cell with a nutter. One guy set fire to his mattress and threw himself on it. By the time they got to him he was suffocated.'

Larry says he is clean now. He spends his time fishing and writing — songs and poems. He has written a ballad about the rose garden in Preston Park, and many Country-and-Western style lyrics: a vocabulary of freight trains, coyotes, tumbleweed and moving on. The Country-and-Western sensibility of high emotion, nostalgia and root-lessness speaks to people like Larry far more than any British cultural tradition can. His worst enemy is solitude; his greatest fear, of dying like the man they called Snowy, who was found dead last Saturday night in the town centre.

Colin is thirty-eight, and comes from the Rhondda. He wears a donkey jacket, a woollen hat, jeans and heavy-duty boots. He stands in a corner of the hall at a makeshift easel, to which is pinned a large sheet of white paper. As the afternoon wears on, a Nordic landscape emerges — pine forests, frozen river, log-hut. He is used to oils rather than water colours. The colours are mainly Prussian blue and pale blue. When he colours the moon a silvery gold and stains the snow with its reflected light, it doesn't quite work as it should. Colin is a sensitive man; intense brown eyes and warm smile. He has always been able to paint, even when he was at school, but no one encouraged him. He was destined for the pits, as his father had been; but when he was sixteen he left the valley and has never been back. 'There was nothing to keep me there.'

Colin has worked all over Britain; and was in fact a miner at Grimethorpe. He left through what they called 'natural wastage', although as he says, 'what the pits do to a man's body is bloody unnatural wastage.' He came South and worked on a sewerage scheme in Brighton, an eight-foot bore, one and a half miles under the sea. 'That was heavy work. We drank a lot of Guinness, smoked best Afghan hash, the only way to make it bearable.'

In 1971 he had tuberculosis, and spent some months in a sanatorium in Devon. There, he practised painting. 'They wanted me to do GCEs, qualify for Art School. But I never had the confidence in myself. When I recovered I came back to Brighton and worked as a lifeguard on the beach. It was too late for anything else by then.

'I went to Holland and Sweden, labouring, painting. Always to cold places. I'd like to go somewhere warm, where the light and the colours are different. I'm living in a bed-and-breakfast place, £45 a week. It's squalid, dirty, I can't paint there. The landlord is only interested in money. I got paid Tuesday, skint by Friday. This is the only place that doesn't cost money; there's not many of them left.

'In Sweden I met a woman. We lived together for six years, three of them married. Then suddenly it was over. Oh, she was beautiful. Everything about those years was magic. I never thought it was possible that men should ever see such beauty. I always knew I didn't deserve it; but when it ended, it was like a knife in the flesh. Her father had been a champion driver of a twelve-dog sleigh, huskies. I've driven a three-dog sleigh, the way they move over the snow, it's out of this world. We used to walk the countryside, the light, the air, the emptiness — it belongs to you. They have these stugers, wooden huts in the middle of nowhere, where you can stay the night if the snow or mist comes down. They're not locked, and nobody vandalises them. Here, they'd be wrecked. People respect nature there.

'When it was over, it broke me up. I came back to England and had to go to an asylum. After that, your life can never be the same again. It's made me turn against the obsession with work and money: labouring, living in digs, getting pissed. Life is more than that. All I'd like is a roof over my head, somewhere I could paint. What I have is a gift; not to be squandered earning money.'

Colin takes a sketch pad from a plastic carrier bag: pencil drawings of people who come to the Centre: some sitting bolt upright at tables, others slumped in postures of defeat. There is a delicate sketch of a naked man and woman embracing in a meadow. He says 'I suppose that is my fantasy, wishful thinking. To be held like that. Once you've known it, to have it taken away is hard to bear. It means you daren't let yourself go with anyone, ever again.'

Colin is a talented, wounded man. He speaks of the randomness of fate; how people's life situations bear no resemblance to their worth. 'I don't mind other people being rich', he says, 'but I wish they wouldn't expect everybody else to be like them.'

Kevin says that he would never use the Centre; but then he stops, thinks and says 'Never's a long time.' He has pink spiky hair, a worn leather jacket with studs and chains, jeans that have frayed into open gashes above the knee, scuffed black boots. He is 19. He came down from Middlesbrough in the autumn of 1986 to look for a job. When he got here, he found he was too late for the temporary Christmas work; or perhaps, as he admitted, employers didn't like the look of him. 'I wouldn't make a very good Father Christmas, I might scare the children.' He complains of prejudice — 'Just because I'm a punk' — as though his appearance were an accident of birth rather than a chosen image. When I put this to him, he disagreed. 'No, this is me. This is what I am.' It is clearly a question of identity. 'Why do they only look at the surface?' And indeed, he has a good-natured smile and a self-mocking sense of humour. He says 'I should have worked in the shipyards. Only they couldn't wait for me, they closed down before I got there.' He is sleeping on the floor of a friend's flat. He went to Social Security several times, but nothing came through. 'It was such a hassle, I had to start begging.' He goes to London, does the tube and railway stations. 'You can earn more in less time than they keep you waiting at the Social.' He says he can make forty or fifty pounds a day, especially in the pre-Christmas period.

He is one of those who have disappeared from the unemployment register; part of the 'success story' of bringing down the figures. He suggests that begging and private alms-giving might be the answer to the breakdown of the benefits system. 'Privatisation. People moaning about their taxes being given to those who don't deserve it. They can give it direct. Tough shit if you're an old tramp covered in sores but for women who take their babies and sit outside the big shops, they'd make a bomb. You have to learn to know the crowd — it's a bit of a roulette-wheel. You can spot those who'll pay up. You don't bother with those in a hurry or dressed up too smart. It's the faces you have to look at — easy-going, kind-hearted or just guilty. I wonder Thatcher hasn't thought of it already. Private Social Security. Dial-a-beggar.' Homeless men are not quite the caricature of the popular imagination. Far from being inadequate individuals — although there are doubtless some — behind the personal story of most of them is the shadow of vast socially and economically determined events; the most enduring and conspicuous of which is that profound change of function in the lives of many of those who used to be called working class.

The triumph of the Right

Many people feel that there is something wrong with the way we live at a level deeper than anything that reaches public or political debate; it remains an obscure intuition, a rather formless apprehension that the patterns of development of our society are not sustainable indefinitely, and that all the pollutants and contaminants are not merely by-products of industrial society but an integral part of it. They are equally aware that traditional socialist formulations do not touch this deeper malaise either. But because all political discussion shifts on the pitifully fixed arc between Left and Right, they turn away from politics, however unquiet and dissatisfied they feel. Because so much socialist rhetoric and ambition has not been critical of the implications of capitalist wealth-creation, but has for the most part merely dreamed of applying the sometimes strange fruits of those processes in a more humane way, socialism has implicitly underwritten, or at best failed to engage with, some of the malign effects and consequences of industrial society. And these are not simply to be observed in something external called 'the environment', but are reflected in the lives of individuals, in violence and disorders, a more profound sickness and unhappiness than anything traditional socialists have any prescription for. Such people are waiting for an analysis that comprehends and illuminates their anxieties, and for accounts of the world that comprehend their pain and will transcend the sterility of existing discussion. Just as people wonderingly said in the early years of the twentieth century as they were for the first time exposed to the passionate oratory of the pioneer socialists 'I've been a socialist all my life without realizing it', so the same is true of people today who, if the debates were not rigidly constructed along existing polarities, would discover that the more urgent and humane appeals of the Green movement correspond to what they have been thinking and feeling.

In the meantime, the popular imagination is securely colonized by the politics of impotence and despair.

Alec, from Bridgeton in the centre of Glasgow. A member of the committee of the local community centre, he works for the Pensioners' Federation, and has always been a committed political activist. Now seventy-six, he is a small man with flat cap and raincoat, wrinkled face with bright alert eyes. Most of his life he worked delivering milk in the central area of the city. He was born one of nine children in a cavernous sandstone tenement in Bridgeton. As he speaks, he evokes the smoke and grime of the buildings in a Glasgow where the sky scarcely lightened between November and February, where people suffered from TB and malnutrition. His family lived in two rooms, a kitchen with a recess for his parents' bed, while all the children slept in the other room. When each new baby came along, its bed was the bottom drawer of the cupboard. The next one moved up a drawer. 'Then we went into the bed for the little 'uns. When you got to be about nine, you had to be separated, so there was a boys' bed and a girls' bed. There was hardly room for any other furniture. It was a high room, like a cave. Always cold. My father was a brush-maker all his life. They made wire brushes; later the bristles were stuck into tar but they came out too easily. He never earned enough to keep his family.

'The Labour Party was the best thing that ever happened to the working class', says Alec, who was a member and a passionate campaigner. 'But then it all went sour. When? With Harold Wilson. Everything went wrong. All this permissiveness, look at it. The only way the young women know they'll ever get a house is to have a wain. So they do, just to get a roof over their head. Woman's place is to look after her family and the home. Women going out to work, it's all wrong. There's no discipline. When I was a boy, the local policeman would fetch you one the side of the head if you were doing wrong. They daren't now.

'The Labour Party has wrecked this city. Pulling down

the old buildings, they should have done them up, instead of putting people in hutches, cages outside the city. The Labour Party has all these militants, they'll never get in power again, they've gone too far from the people. I think Maggie's got it right. Of course, Enoch Powell warned about all this crime in Birmingham and Manchester. We haven't got black people in Glasgow. We have a few Pakistanis, but they're hardworking, they don't drink and smoke and they believe in keeping their women at home. We welcome them. We can respect them.

'But the whole world's been ruined. It isn't like it was, and it's the Labour Party to blame. I got disillusioned. But give the Conservatives a few years, they'll put a stop to people scrounging, all the layabouts spending the day in bed, just dragging themselves downstairs to pick up their Giro. I don't say it's their fault, it's the system that pays them more money to lay in bed than to go to work. Then of course they lose the will to do anything. They advertise all these jobs in *The Herald*, they can't get the workers. People get too much money for doing nothing, it saps their strength and their will. We knew we had to get up and work or we didn't eat.'

Alec is one of a generation whose eyes remain fixed on the poverty and humiliations and suffering of an earlier industrial experience. Many of his generation have seen what appears to be a steady improvement in the system; and if that system nevertheless seems not to be working as well as it should, this must be the fault of lazy or uncooperative individuals, a consequence of indiscipline and permissiveness rather than of mutations in the system itself. His story of disillusionment with the Labour Party is widely shared. What the Labour Party experiences as apathy is in fact the process of emotional withdrawal, of puzzlement and despair. There seems to be nowhere to go for the ingrown radicalism of people like Alec. That he should have taken the dramatic step of leaving the Labour Party and embracing Thatcherism with such fervour, particularly in Glasgow, is a source of some disagreement and amused tolerance by those with whom he works in the community. Yet it is a path that has been followed by many others in Britain. It is as though all other outlets are blocked; and once you become aware of the epic inadequacy of Labour to respond to the issues of the age, it seems there is nowhere else to go. Most people simply become detached from politics, and retreat into private life, there to wrestle as individuals with all the unresolved social conflicts they think they have abandoned, but more and more see the rhetoric of the Right as liberating — blame the people for the failings of the social and economic order. The severance of social evils from the system that delivers the economic goods is the secret of the triumph of the Right; so that all the unhappy consequences of violence, addictions, loneliness, crime, despair, break-up of human bondings and solidarities are collusively separated from the appeals to greed and promises of enhanced personal wealth, instead of being seen as part of the price paid for all the benefits that have been conceded on the terms of capitalism.

There could be no clearer demonstration of the need to open up a pathway through the impasse, so that former radicals and members of the Labour Party don't see the alternatives simply as alienation from politics or taking the broad and easy highway to Conservatism, that by now well-beaten path. The silences and evasions, the elisions and confusion (how many people say they feel confused!) cover that terrain which the Greens should be ploughing with such assiduity. The support is there, but has not yet been articulated in ways that connect with people's experience. The Green call to liberation has greater resonance to the poor than to even the most convinced environmentalist, the most committed organic farmer, the most anguished and guilt-ridden consumer of luxuries from the Third World.

The truth that human beings cannot live by bread alone has been obscured by the obstruction of an even more obvious truth — that without bread we perish. It is the exploitation of this latter that has dazzled us in the over-elaboration by capitalism of its material products. This process has been rendered the more opaque and impenetrable by the lesson assimilated by capitalism from the materialist philosophy of a socialism whose greatest contribution turns out to have been in the realm of the spirit rather than in that of the material, to which it once laid such extravagant claim.

CHAPTER THREE

The making of the transnational working class

Just as people have been evicted from what they thought were settled ways of living in the industrial societies of the West, so the same thing is happening all over the countries of the South, to people who have been engaged for as long as they can remember in agriculture. One of the consequences of the 'green revolution' of the 1960s has been the expense of sustaining it, not only in terms of fertilizer and pesticide, but also in terms of use of scarce water supplies and of exhaustion of the land. This has meant that only the richer farmers can afford to continue, and that large numbers of small and marginal farmers either become landless labourers or leave for the cities.

'In India, drinking water scarcity, unknown till the early seventies except in the Rajasthan desert, has now become a routine feature of the rural reality in two-thirds of the country. Meanwhile, the green revolution's motor force — the irrigation pump — continues to be active, drawing enormous quantities of water to feed heavy-yielding varieties of crops and generate profits for the prosperous peasant in the 'food bowls.'

'The causes of this degradation of the land are not difficult to discern: organised disruption of the balanced system of agriculture, forestry and pasturing that once existed in the country; relentless deforestation; neglect of soil and water conservation measures, rampant growth of monoculture and disappearance of genetic diversity; and the calculated disruption of watersheds by large irrigation projects, which tend to concentrate water collected from a huge area in a tiny pocket, impoverishing the bulk of the watershed in order to irrigate the fields of the well-off peasantry in the small pocket.

'One major result of all this has been the disruption of the normal rainfall pattern in region after region, although an absolute decrease in total precipitation has tended to be rare. This disruption affects crops at critical stages in their growth cycle and tells on their yields'. (Praful Bidwai, *Times of India*, February 1988).

People displaced from traditional agriculture by these processes either become landless labourers or they migrate. Most go to the nearest big town or the State capital, but more and more are going further afield — to the Gulf, to Singapore, Europe and America. With a single and increasingly 'rationalized' world market, national barriers are more and more an impediment to economic growth. George Ball, former US Under-secretary of State and chairman of Lehmann Brothers International has gone as far as to say 'Working through great Corporations that straddle the earth, men are able for the first time to utilise world resources with an efficiency dictated by the objective logic of profit. By contrast, the nation-state is a very old-fashioned idea and badly adapted to our present complex world.'

Those who have been drawn from rural societies in the countries of the South into the labour process of the rich societies of Western Europe must undergo a violent reshaping of the sensibility. It is painful enough to have to leave the familiar home-place (and in spite of all the prejudice of the rich that the poor go to the big cities in search of 'bright lights' or an 'easy life', it is necessity that drives them there); but to travel half way round the world for the privilege of work as domestic servant or factory worker is a cruel and wounding experience. One of the reasons why people from India and elsewhere have continued to come to Britain in spite of racist immigration laws and high unemployment is that the extended family system of such migrants enables them to take work at wages that would not support nuclear families; the tradition of joint family income and pooled resources serves the employers of factory workers in Britain's dwindling, though still substantial manufacturing sector.

Keralans in Croydon

In the Northern (and poorer) part of the Conservative borough of Croydon, there is a significant community of people who come from Kerala, one of the smaller states of India, comprising a little over one percent of the land mass, and with a population of twenty-five million. It has a coastline of 600 kilometres, and some of the most spectacular beaches in India, as the presence of a few of those stragglers from the 1960s, escapees from Western materialism, testifies; ageing now, they sit smoking on the silver sand under the palm trees, dreaming their faintly archaic dreams of transcendence. The palms, with the tangle of green coconuts that yield up to six harvests a year, are the most prominent crop; together with plantain, clusters of red, yellow and green bananas, they create an impression all over Kerala of luxuriance and great natural beauty; although the lives of those who live in their shade are far from idyllic.

For one thing, there is one of the highest rates of unemployment in India; a fact which the recently elected (1987) Leftist coalition State government can do little to alter. Officially, almost three million people are without work, and this certainly understates the real figure, for it doesn't include those who are employed only casually or underemployed. Above all, it takes no account of what is the State's most poignant export — its people. Kerala's export of its young men and their labour earn for it the reputation of a 'remittance economy'; that variant of the trade in human flesh which the modern world finds acceptable, indeed indispensable.

At Trivandrum airport, you have the most vivid encounter with this sad traffic. The barriers hold back the crush of people each day, the women, old people and children waiting to see their men depart for Bombay, the Gulf, Singapore, Britain, Canada and the USA. Lone men in neatly pressed trousers and sober shirts, symbolically having shed the traditional lunghi — the cotton wrap that they hold so elegantly between thumb and forefinger as they walk through the dusty villages and small towns. As the airbus takes off, the people move forward: solemn children, women, some of them crying, the old, wondering if they will ever see their sons again. The viewing area of the airport is a mass of bright sarees and black umbrellas. On the plane to Kerala, I sat between a tailor working in Bombay and a hotel worker from Bahrain. Both are making the annual journey home. 'You feel sad because your children don't really know you. But what to do? What choice do we have?' One day, they'll have enough money to return, build a house, give the children a good education.

And they do return; bearing twin-tub washers, TV and tape recorders, household appliances, fridges and videos. The unloading of the returnees' cargo makes the baggage reclaim area look like the warehouse of a vast department store. And many do indeed build their own houses. 'Gulf money', and transfers from Bombay or the UK have rearranged the pattern of life in Kerala for tens of thousands of families. New houses with marble walls, mosaic and ceramic tiling, painted maroon and ochre and white, with ruby electric doorbells and wrought-iron window bars can be found in the smallest towns and villages, incongruous against palm and cocoa-trees, and making the palm-leaf huts of the poor and landless appear even more faded and fragile. Those who return may extend the family plot, turning wetland to copra production; or they may buy a private transport bus, a taxi or autorickshaw; some open a small 'hotel' — a tea-stall with dry snacks and a few wooden benches. During the years of recession and uncertainty in the Gulf, the contracts have been drying up. Many have come back for good and found that there is nothing for them to do. They sell their houses, their consumer goods, and are then reduced to the condition that drove them abroad in the first place. Only there is nowhere left to go, unless they want to take their chances on the pavements of Bombay or Madras. Migration has become far harder; and in the familiar terms of an argument heard worldwide now, it is claimed that Indian workers have been pricing themselves out of the Middle East labour market. They are being replaced as construction workers and labourers by Bangladeshis and South Koreans who, it is said, will work longer hours and for less pay than their Indian counterparts.

There are other consequences of money remitted from abroad. In Connemara Market in Trivandrum, the poor have always bargained with the vendors over the price of basic commodities — bananas, rice, oil, fruit. The new rich never have time for such subtleties, and pay the asking price without questioning it. As a result, the vendors ask more, prices rise and place even essentials out of reach of the poor. And then, most of the money that has come back here has not been productively invested. For the most part, it has gone on conspicuous consumption, which means imports. The luxury shops in Trivandrum are full of ornamental light fittings, Western drugs, foodstuffs, cosmetics and household goods.

But at least those who have gone to Bombay and the Gulf can return. For others who have gone further afield, migration is not so easily reversed, although they try to visit their home village at least once every two or three years.

Cherayinkil is a small town some forty kilometres from Trivandrum, and is the home of some of the Malayali-speaking community in North Croydon. With its placid lakes and irrigated paddy-fields, its palm-groves, the little shops with sacks of rice, rolls of cloth and clusters of red bananas, the railway track that bisects the town, and the palms which almost meet high above the streets in a green Gothic architecture, it could not contrast more starkly with the buff-coloured brick, grey skies and sodium street-lamps of the late Victorian suburb. In Cherayinkil, I visited the home of a family whose experience of migration has been characteristic: of the family of eight children, three have been to the Gulf and come home, one is in Bombay and two are in Britain. The oldest brother is lucky — he has a job with the State Agricultural Service. He lives with his wife and three children in an old house with pale yellow plaster walls, a courtyard with a few plantains and a cow-shed. Opposite his house, a new villa is being constructed: women walk by, bearing huge slabs of marble on their head, heavier than their own body weight.

Radhakrishnan has been able to put his agricultural expertise to practical use, and has extended the few acres of family land that were so inadequate to provide a living for all the children. He is proud of his plantation of new coconut trees. They have been properly manured and raised up on mounds; the water from a nearby lake has been used for irrigation in such a way that the water does not stagnate, but remains in constant movement. The trees have been treated against pests, and will yield after only four years. We go through the field where the paddy has dried out, and the thick stubble offers evidence that the harvest was good. In the clearings, landless families (and 52 per cent of the people of Kerala have no land) sit in the afternoon heat, dark and watchful beside their rudimentary thatched shelter, with their few battered utensils, their half-dozen hens, a dog and a goat. They depend entirely on their work as casual and day labourers. The sun glints on the palm-fronds, and the leaves chatter noisily in the humid breeze. A huge cloud, pink from the setting sun, fills the fields with a strange coppery light. In the temple square, on the other side of the field, a festival is taking place. The temple is festooned with lights, and people crowd the booths and stalls which are selling incense sticks, coconuts and rose water, bangles, fabrics, sweets and holy pictures.

Ramabhadran, Radhakrishnan's brother, works in a

factory in Croydon, on permanent night shift, making plastic pots. On Friday nights he meets with some of his friends in the front room of a neglected bay-windowed house: a sparsely furnished and sombre place, with two single beds, a dressing table and a sofa with foam cushions. The walls are brightened by Malayali calendars and paintings. Rajan and his family rent this house for £60 a week. Rajan works at Philips, his brother in a factory assembling refrigeration plant. They have just bought a run-down house in a neighbouring street. Friends are helping with the renovation — wiring, plumbing, plastering, joinery and decoration, all on a mutual help basis, which draws on practices of pooled skills and resources from the pre-cash economy of their home place.

Ravi came to Croydon three years ago, when he was eighteen. He had to leave his studies at university in Trivandrum for factory work at Southern Coolers. His brother works in a Kentucky Fried Chicken take-away.

Many of the jobs that migrants are doing in Britain are similar to work that can be seen in India — indeed, some of the multinationals like Philips have a presence in both countries. If the people from Kerala take low-paid jobs, this is not, as the myth runs, because British people wouldn't do them. It is that the British nuclear family could not live on the low wages. With three or four adults working, it is possible to live on shared resources. In this way, the multinationals have been able to draw upon older family traditions of people from the Third World in order to 'pioneer' new low wages in non-unionised firms in Western Europe. The idea of 'becoming competitive in the world' takes on real significance, when you can see the beginnings of a truly integrated international division of labour, where workers in Bombay or Manila are competing against workers in Croydon for the same jobs.

Sunil sits on the candlewick bedspread, nursing his young niece, Vini. Two years ago his sister went to Kerala to get married. Her husband has been refused even a visitor's visa to Britain; the closest she can get to him is to watch the video of her wedding over and over again. She does not know when he will see his daughter. The punitive entry conditions for other members of the family actually work against the possibility of the family surviving on the low wages they receive. So the exhortations of the Conservative government about 'pricing ourselves into jobs "(not to mention its rhetoric about the sanctity of the family) sound both hypocritical and impossible of realization.

These young men all remained in work even through the worst of the recession, although they have all been made redundant at least once. They have yielded to the demand that their labour be flexible, they have taken jobs at lower wages with exemplary self-denial. This has exposed them to all kinds of humiliations, insults to their intelligence, racial abuse and harassment, exploitation. Some of the first words they learnt when they came to work in the factories were 'Piss off', 'black bastard', 'fucking cunt'. They say that even though they had been taught English at school, they were shy of speaking at first, and had certainly never heard words like that. The choices before them were of over-educated idleness in Kerala, or under-use of their intelligence, and material comfort in London; both forms of violence and impoverishment.

All belong to the formerly untouchable Ezheva caste, the largest single group in Kerala, who make up about a quarter of the population. They were lifted up through education by Shri Narayana Guru at the turn of the century. One of the consequences of this — combined with a number of progressive Left State governments since the 1950s — is that Kerala has one of the highest literacy rates in India. Highly educated unemployed people have a greater impulse to travel great distances in search of work. They are well aware that their labour in Croydon proletarianizes them, but any work is better than none. It is simply that the better life they had anticipated is attended by so many unforeseen disadvantages; and reconciling all the contradictions can be achieved only by keeping alive the dream of return, that sustenance of all first-generation migrants who believe they can reverse the irreversible.

But not a return empty-handed; nor a return on anybody else's terms. The only way to go home would be if they had saved some money. Otherwise, their fate would be that of those who have remained in Kerala. There, the principal employment is in copra, fishing, cashew-nuts and coir (coconut fibre), rubber, and palm-plantations and quarrying. And the conditions in which these workers must labour makes the industrial employment of Bombay or Croydon far more desirable.

There are about 200 000 quarry-workers in Kerala. The road from Trivandrum to the coast is flanked by groups of workers, many of them women and children, cross-legged beside a heap of grey boulders, with only a single dry palm-leaf propped against the stones to provide shelter from the searing sun. The excavation of the quarries has scooped great artificial cliffs in the landscape. A stream of trucks takes loads of boulders to the roadside where the stone-breakers sit, eight, ten hours at a time, like the inhabitants of some vast penal colony. Before them is a stone anvil, on which they place the rocks, which it is their job to break with a small sharp hammer into regular pieces of equal size — some ¾inch, some ½inch, some 1½inches. The hazards of their work are dust-induced diseases, TB, bronchitis and lung disorders. The air is filled with a metallic music of tapping and hammering, the rhythm of unceasing labour, as the big stones are fragmented into the sizes required for house-building or road construction. The workers are exposed to the fierce bleaching sun, the fumes from lorries, buses and scooters; their faces are pale with stone dust. Beside them stands a metal tiffin-can and a water-jug. A hunchback boy of about 15 sits between two women, one of them in her sixties, so thin that her stringy arms seem barely to have the strength to lift the hammer; the other woman is seven or eight months pregnant. A woman carries a head-load of finished stones to the steadily growing pile; she needs two men to help lift the basket onto her head. Male workers are paid 20 Rupees a day (about £1), women get 15 Rupees. If several members of a family work together, their combined income will provide a reasonable living: The characteristic house is of wood and plaster, has a concrete floor; many own a radio, a bicycle, a watch, an electric fan. These workers have been unionised, organised by the CPI(M); but they are still employed by contractors who act as go-betweens for the private owners of the quarries. In this way, many workers remain in ignorance of their rights: they may not know that they can claim against negligent employers for injury and sickness. One family had been cheated of compensation when the father had been killed in a landslip in the quarry.

The other principal industries in the State are coir, employing almost a million people, and cashew nuts (half a million — most of the cashew crop goes for export; cashew workers were formerly employed in factories by the government, but the former Congress (I) government abolished the monopoly, so that private merchants could buy in the free market. Now contractors buy the cashews, and employ people in their own homes at low wages. Shelling the cashews is semi-skilled work — you have to open the nuts without breaking the brittle kernels.) There are about 100 000 bamboo workers, half a million engaged in fishing, and perhaps a further million in other artisan employment. Middle-income groups — shopkeepers, middlemen and merchants — constitute about twelve per cent of the population. There are currently 100 000 Keralans in the Gulf, and many thousands more elsewhere in India and in other parts of the world.

Trivandrum, with its half-million people, is far from the European idea of a city, in spite of the imposing government buildings and its ubiquitous churches. St Thomas the Apostle preached in Kerala in the First century AD; and the presence of a Christian enclave in India has, over the years, drawn many more recent comers than the Syrian Church: Catholics, Protestants, the Church of South India and twentieth century American evangelicals are all prominent. They have their redbrick or white-painted churches in the centre of the city; but this impressive architecture, Gothic, Early English, Byzantine, soon fades into narrow streets and winding lanes, small markets and palm-shaded courtyards, cramped shops and booths, and pavement-vendors. The substantial villas give way to sun-dried hutments that will not even withstand the onset of the summer rains.

But the most significant story from Kerala, and most characteristic of the impoverishing effects of Western-inspired patterns of development everywhere, is the fate of the fishing industry, on which hundreds of thousands of people along the coast have traditionally depended. The fishing communities around Trivandrum were converted to Christianity by Francois Xavier in the sixteenth century, and remain Catholic; those around Quilon are predominantly Hindu, while Muslims dominate the Calicut area. The fishing people of the Trivandrum district have always lived in huddled villages on the shore — sadly inturned and often wretched places, in dramatic contrast to the openness of sea and sky. They have always made a contribution to their church from the daily catch of fish, and have been systematically exploited both by moneylenders in the finance of the fishing, and by auctioneers in selling the fish.

Fishing was formerly carried out from plank canoes, dugouts and catamarans — logs of soft wood tied together with coir ropes. The fish was auctioned by middlemen to the vendors — women head-loaders with baskets reminiscent of Hogarth's shrimp-girl — and to men on cycles who pedalled through the countryside. Most of the fishing was done on a credit basis; and in the rainy season when the catches are small, the fishermen became dependent on credit at very high rates of interest, with the result that they were never free of debt.

82

Government reforms and international aid — often with the best intentions — have made the lives of the poor fishing communities far worse. Mechanized trawlers which were provided to improve the catch and the working conditions inevitably came into the hands of the rich, who alone could afford to maintain and deploy them. These entrepreneurs wanted to catch only the most profitable fish, especially those that could be exported — prawns for the markets of Japan, Europe and the USA. Although intended for deep-sea fishing, these trawlers fished indiscriminately in traditional inshore waters, on which the fishing communities had depended for their livelihood. Even as the catches of fish grew, and a certain number of jobs were provided in freezing and processing plants on the coast, more and more fishing families were being dispossessed. The money generated by more 'efficient' fishing did not find its way into the hands of those whose whole way of living was being undermined. In fact, the trawlers only wanted the big prawns, which involved ploughing the sea-bed and disturbing the ecosystem. For one kilo of prawns, the trawlers catch fifty kilos of other fish; thirty or forty per cent of this is small fish, which die immediately. This is made into fish-meal and exported for fertilizer.

In the Community Programme Office in Trivandrum, a modest concrete building behind a new office-block, Aleyamma Vijayana and Eugene Cujas, who have been working with the fishing communities to get mechanized trawling banned, articulate the people's anger. 'We export precious protein to feed the overfed, while half the people in Kerala suffer protein deficiency. The calorie intake of the average Indian is 1900 a day. In the USA it is twice as much. And then they send us charitable food to make up for what they have taken out of the mouths of the poor.'

The encroachment of industrialized fishing on traditional workers has made what was already a hard life intolerable. The cause of the fishing people was taken up initially by some Catholic priests and nuns working in the communities. They did so against the express wishes of the church hierarchy. A Catholic nun went on hunger-strike to draw attention to the plight of the fishing people. She was persuaded to give up only because there was a fear that if she died there would be violence. The Kerala government set up a study committee on the banning of trawlers; after two years, its report voted seven to six against the ban; but since so many members of the committee depended upon the State government for their jobs, it was not exactly the most impartial of judgments. The agitation continued, and the government was persuaded to set up another committee, from outside Kerala, including scientists end ecologists.

Ms Vijayana says the government is interested only in fast modernisation to boost foreign earnings. 'They need the money to import luxuries for the rich. We have been examining ways in which the lives of traditional fishing communities can be made easier — on-board engines, for instance, fibre-glass boats. Of course the trawler owners will fight — they are the wealthiest most powerful people in Kerala, plantation owners, government bureaucrats, film stars. They're not interested in conservation, either of people's livelihood or of the ecosystem. The day's profit is all that matters to them. The trawlers and freezing plants make sure that none of the wealth generated goes to the fishermen who live here; that money is used to buy atomic power or Western high technology.'

The feeling is widespread among Indian radicals that colonialism lives on in ways more subtle than conquest and military subjugation. It is present in aid and charity, as well as in the control of patents and specialisms by transnational companies, in the genetic engineering of high-yielding crops that depend upon expensive inputs from the West, in development schemes that are predestined to benefit only the rich. 'The Keralan People's Science Movement is fighting against deforestation, dam-building, drugs that are dumped in India. You can go into any pharmacy in Trivandrum and buy drugs that are banned in your country. We are fighting against Gulf money that is frittered away in conspicuous consumption, foreign exchange that is used up to import sophisticated machinery that will put people out of work, while we export our people to do demeaning labour in the countries of the rich.'

On Cherayinkil station, a young man gives me the address of a cousin in Newham; somebody else produces a page torn from a notebook with a name and telephone number in Croydon. An old man has not heard from his son in Birmingham. The train to Trivandrum is late. The Bangalore express races past. Suddenly, there is a power-cut and all the lights go out; in the warm darkness, hundreds of small torches glow like fireflies. Radhakrishnan waits until the train eventually arrives. There are a few last messages for the family — what about his sister's marriage? Has Bhadran got over his operation? He had written to say he was ill and wanted to come home; their father had been an ayurvedic doctor, and Bhadran had felt unhappy in the impersonal and mechanized atmosphere of Croydon hospital.

Meanwhile in the South London street, the curtains are drawn while the Malayali films play on the video — Kumatty, Elipattayam, with their evocation of the light and colour of the village landscapes. The influences that have driven people from Kerala are a little clearer; but it is impossible to exaggerate the pain of migration: learning to adapt, how to become working class. The passing of the years makes the hope of return burn the more keenly, even as it becomes less and less likely, for the money gets all used up in the survival from day to day.

With time, of course, people do adapt, some more effectively than others. Ravi's father had originally gone to Singapore as a dock labourer, but when there came a threat of expulsion of migrant workers, he returned to Cherayinkil. Because he held a British passport, he had come to Croydon in the 1970s. Within two years of Ravi's arrival he died, and Ravi at twenty-two found himself head of the family, feeling the responsibility of looking after his mother and young brother. He worked hard, after four years, got a better job in a factory that was almost all-white. This lasted no more than six weeks. There was another worker from Kerala in the factory, who was accepted as the sole 'tame Paki', and didn't protest at this role. To have two Malayali-speaking workers was too much for the white work force. They put the pressure on Ravi's colleague, who became hostile towards him. He duly turned against Ravi, and accused him of losing the respect which the white people had shown him, and of putting pressure on his marriage. Ravi felt he had no choice but to leave. He went back to the former place of work, where they welcomed him eagerly enough — in a place of such high turnover of labour, and with such a low level of competence, Ravi's efficiency and conscientious work were valuable contributions. In so many of these small factories the workers feel themselves despised, as they despise the products they make.

Because so many people from Kerala come to Britain as penniless migrants, they have little choice but to do factory work. Very few have money as some of the East African Gujeratis had, and cannot start their own business. As a measure of the violence involved in the reshaping of the sensibility of the people, it is enough to hear Ravi talk lovingly of the traditions and festivals of his home. Speaking of the festival of Onam, he says 'Onam is the new year, when everybody dances and dresses up in their best. The story is that the kingdom was once ruled over by a wise and just king called Mahavili. He was so good and kind to his people that the gods themselves became jealous, and feared that he might become an object of greater reverence than they were. So the god Vishnu went down to earth in the shape of a dwarf. He came to the kingdom of Mahavili, and asked if space could be found for him to lie down, just a small plot of earth, three feet long. The king said of course, he would be most welcome.

But because Vishnu can assume any shape he chooses, he said he would measure out the three feet that had been given to him. His first footstep covered the whole of the long narrow coastal strip that is Kerala. His second covered the sky above it. The wise king recognized whom he was dealing with, and lowered his head. The third foot was to crush him into the earth beneath to the same depth. But before he died, he was allowed one wish. And he wished that he might be allowed to visit his beloved kingdom on one day each year. And ever since, the people of Kerala have always celebrated that day; they have always danced and sung, and feasted and worn their best clothes and been hospitable to strangers, so that they should be fit to receive their lost king, if they should ever come across him.'

British factory life, the culture of the pub, the Sun and racism, is not seen as a liberation by those who are expected to adapt to it.

Ravendra has just returned from six months in Kerala, where he was married. The video of the ceremony is played over and over; the white lunghi and solemn expression of the groom, the red and gold bridal gown, the exchange of ring and necklace, the garlands and the wedding feast for 600 people in the hall in Attingal, while the bride and groom exchange not a word. The drive through the narrow roads of the town in the Padmini cars decorated with tinsel and balloons and the Christmas baubles which Ravendra had taken from England. Then, the separation from the wife, while she goes for her interview with the British authorities in Madras, to convince them that the wedding was not undertaken for the purpose of immigration into Britain. During his return to India, Ravendra, who over the years had adapted to the life of the pub and the factory, became another person, rediscovering his Indianness in the homeplace. He wears his lunghi at home in Croydon now, he has taken to playing the snakeskin finger-drums that he manipulates so expertly, he has become more attentive to his social and religious duties.

His brother, Sunil, in part resolutely resists the culture of the English working class, although outwardly he is the most conformist of all. He will not drink alcohol, he doesn't smoke, he doesn't take part in any out of work activities with the whites he works with. He is determined to succeed and to make money. He has graduated from the shop floor to operating the computer in the factory. He has regularly asked for increases in pay, there being no union; and his money has gone up over three years from £1.85 and hour, through £2.50, to £3.50, and now £3.85. He leaves home early in the morning, and is never late for work. Once there, however, he is compliant and agreeable to his colleagues. He does not rise to racist taunts. They call him Sunny anglicizing his name; and he listens to the obscenities and laughs at the sometimes painful jokes, without ever showing what he really feels. Some of the other Malayali workers call him a white Malayali, while the whites call him Paki. He doesn't rise to the taunts, but keeps his head down and gets on with his work. He absorbs the violence, determined to save up, to go back to Kerala with some money in his pocket and to start a business of his own. He is seen by the Indian workers as having influence with the whites, and they turn to him to intercede for them. He tells how an elderly man from Sri Lanka came to him with tears in his eyes and begged him to get a job for his wife in the wiring section of the factory. He himself, in his late fifties, has cancer, and is becoming too weak to continue working. His young son is no help, spends the money he earns on himself, on his car and on drink. He desperately needs to find work for his wife, so that they can go on paying the mortgage on their house when his health fails completely. Sunil says he will see what he can do; but only he knows how false this perception of his position is. He has no influence at all with the management. He simply submits to the discomfort of getting the worst of both worlds in the interests of his longer-term plan.

Women workers of Ahmedabad

It isn't only those who are drawn into traditional industries, whether in the West or in the South who form the
new global working class: a far more imaginative and
comprehensive understanding of the common interests of
the oppressed and exploited is required than anything that
national labour movements have so far shown themselves
capable of.

Ahmedabad, with its two and a half million people, is
the sixth city of India. A centre of the textile industry, it
is a spectacular place: within the old walled city, ornate
buildings with intricate traditional Gujerati carving in
wood and stone open out into irregular squares of small
workshops, improvised markets and busy water stand-
pipes. The Sabarmati River opens up an exhilarating sense
of space through the city, even though by March, when
the temperature already touches 40deg. C, its water has
dwindled to a sluggish polluted trickle, and its banks are
dry sand dunes, home to the squatters who continue to
arrive each day from the rural hinterland.

Dariapur is a district of chawls and hutments, an established slum in the centre of the city. The dust, in constant
movement, creates vivid orange sunsets. Cycles and auto-
rickshaws become locked in traffic jams as people go to
and from work in the mills, mills which predictably earned
Ahmedabad the name of the Manchester of India.

The open channels of foul water run between the
houses; offal and detritus lie in the passageways too
narrow to be called streets. The low roofs of Bangalore
tiles and corrugated iron frayed and ragged with rust
almost meet across the crooked pathways; even though
inside, the houses are scrupulously clean, colour-washed
in pale blue and green, while outside the sunlight bleaches
everything it touches.

In Dariapur live many of the tens of thousands of poor
women whose lives have, in recent years, been transformed

by one of the most inspiring feminist initiatives anywhere in the world.

It may not appear like this to those seeing for the first time the homes of the bidi-rollers, chindi-makers, charkha workers, ribbon-makers, potters, supari-makers, blacksmiths or vegetable sellers. But by organizing the formerly powerless against the middlemen and monopolists who have always controlled their conditions of work and payment, Ela Bhatt's Self-Employed Women's Association (the acronym means 'service' in several Indian languages), their income has in many cases doubled, and they have been released from subordination to the (male) moneylenders and merchants who have traditionally dictated the terms of their employment.

Ela Bhatt is now an MLA. Three years ago she was awarded the Swedish Right Livelihood prize; and her office — a plain three-storey building by the narrow iron-work Ellis Bridge — is bright with posters of the Green Party from Germany, and awards from India, Scandinavia and the United States.

The idea of being self-employed in India does not carry the overtones of choice and privilege that it bears in the West (however illusory that may be), but evokes the informal sector, those who are among the very poorest and most oppressed.

SEWA broke away from the Textile Labour Association in 1981, after Ela Bhatt sided with the Untouchables in an outbreak of anti-reservation violence*; although she had been organizer of the women's wing of TLA since 1955. She acknowledges her debt to the older union, and she has sought to retain its original, Gandhian inspiration. In her native Gujarati, she electrifies audiences; and even in English her passion and power come through. 'SEWA is essentially about trade unionism. It has shown that those believed to be beyond the reach of organization because

---

* Protests by higher caste people against the policy of the government reserving a certain number of posts for those from the scheduled castes.

there is no direct employer can combine to improve their condition.' Indeed, when you consider the growth of forms of self-employment for women in Britain — all the home-workers, the stitchers and machinists, toymakers, card-folders, those doing assembly work, electronics and soldering it may be that Ela Bhatt's work has resonance for many women workers in the West.

'The purpose of trade unionism is not only for agitation. It is about solidarity and development. Eighty-nine per cent of women workers in Ahmedabad are self-employed. If they are excluded from the labour movement, you are cutting off the vast majority of workers, and those who most need protection.'

There are three main kinds of female labour: home-based artisans and piece-workers; petty vendors, head-loaders, and, increasingly, power-loom workers; and service workers, including manual labourers, agricultural and construction workers. They have traditionally been constrained by their lack of control over their raw materials and means of labour, as well as by the power of those to whom they sell. The vegetable sellers, for instance, used to borrow 50 Rupees each morning from a moneylender, in order to buy their head-load of tomatoes, oranges or onions, and then repay 55 Rupees at the end of the day. The cane-workers were earning as little as 4 or 5 Rupees a day because their products were homely and unsophisticated and could reach only the poorest markets. The Untouchable waste-paper pickers would work up to twelve hours a day, and were obliged to sell their pickings to a middleman who made big profits by selling in bulk to factories for recycling. There were other problems too: bamboo workers had no space in their huts to manipulate the long canes, and they inevitably encroached on the public areas outside, where they were harassed by the police. As the traditional market-place at Manikchowk required more room to accommodate the bigger stallholders, modern shops and increasing traffic, the vegetable vendors were excluded. ("The authorities said they looked untidy', says Ela Bhatt indignantly; 'as though the traffic were more beautiful than our women'.) It also meant that people were denied the chance to buy cheaper produce, because the women always sold at a lower price than the big dealers. They were refused licences, their vegetables were trampled underfoot by the police if they failed to bribe them. One of the early triumphs of SEWA was a petition to the Supreme Court on behalf of the vegetable sellers, some of whom had been in Manikchowk for several generations. They organized a campaign with the slogan 'Do tokri ki jagah' — space for two basket-loads — and the right of women to pursue their traditional work was upheld.

But the most important task was to provide cheap credit for women. When the banks were approached, they were appalled at the idea of making loans to poor illiterate women with no collateral. Their procedures could not accommodate crowds of work-stained women with their children besieging the counters. Although the banks did eventually provide loans, this was far from being the end of the problem — indeed that was when the real work of SEWA began.

Many women could not repay the loans, either because of their domestic circumstances or because of their limited access to raw materials, their lack of knowledge of the markets, their very low income. The work of organizing the different trades began; of getting unofficial slums reco-gnized so they could be provided with electricity and water to make women's lives easier; of setting up a programme to enhance women's skills and give them opportunities, reach wider markets. SEWA set up its own bank. It is now autonomous, with over 25 000 members, and a lower rate of default than the commercial banks. The average savings are over 400 Rupees (£28).

Similar difficulties occurred when SEWA tried to organize a group insurance scheme for workers. The Life Insurance Company of India was prejudiced against women: they were seen — quite rightly — as a high risk.

The most common cause of death was in childbirth; while out of the 4100 children born to members in the first few years, 561 were either stillborn or died within three years. Many women had to be back at work a few days, indeed sometimes a few hours, after giving birth. A maternity protection scheme is now in operation, offering pre- and post-natal care, and guaranteeing no loss of earnings during the period of confinement.

Of course not all twenty-one trades that have been organized have had the same degree of success. The khol-makers (quilts), who stitch blankets from the waste materials of the mills, formed a co-operative, only to find that the employers would give them only spoilt or oily rags, and even stopped supplying work altogether to women who were the sole breadwinners of the family. SEWA now buys the rags in bulk, distributes them to the quilt-makers and helps market the end product. The waste-paper pickers could not bypass the middlemen, because they had nowhere to store their pickings, while the merchants have big go-downs to accumulate the paper in large quantities. On the other hand, the cart-pullers have succeeded in modifying the design of the traditional heavy handcarts; and the bidi-rollers (the largest group of workers, with over 8 000 members), whose work involves paring away the veins from the tendul-leaves and rolling the tobacco inside, have seen a threefold increase in their earnings since they united against the three monopolists in the city and the ten contractors from whom they buy the leaves and the tobacco.

The conditions in which many women still work are pitiable. The street-sweepers are at risk from TB with the constant inhaling of dust; the fingers of the cotton-pod shellers bleed, and they complain that their menstrual cycle is disturbed by the intensive seasonal labour under the hot sun; the handblock-printers suffer from the effects of the chemicals from which they make their dyes; the firewood-pickers carry loads often greater than their own body weight. The baskets of the head-loaders are reminiscent of the shallows carried by the coster-girls of Mayhew's London, and the carts of the vendors are of the same design as those used in Victorian Britain. One family of bidi-workers included a girl of eight, deftly folding in the ends of the leaves to secure the tobacco inside; and they worked up to twelve hours a day.

The number of women who are the sole supporters of their family varies, according to the different trades, from twenty-nine to forty-one per cent. Their men will have deserted or migrated in search of better work, or are themselves unemployed; they may drink, be sick or disabled. Many of the men are mill-workers thrown out of work by structural changes in the textile industry, or whose lungs have been damaged by long years of exposure to the dust and cotton-waste of the weaving-sheds.

Ela Bhatt: 'We have tried literacy classes, but you know, people are very practical. They learn to read their pass-books, but literacy isn't going to solve the problems of work. It isn't easy for women after a day's labour. It isn't that they have house work — there isn't much of that in poor families. And fuel and feeding the men will help with. But fetching water is exclusively women's work, and that can be arduous if she is a long way from a well or standpipe. In India, women's life expectancy is lower than men's. In the West, of course, it's the other way round.'

Ela Bhatt insists on the trade union function of SEWA. Women have not traditionally seen themselves or been acknowledged as workers; so SEWA is not for discussion of family matters or anything that will reinforce stereotypes. It has brought together all occupations, many of them caste-based. Women integrated as workers act as a powerful solvent of differences, create a kind of solidarity quite new in India. 'For instance, a woman will start talking in public for the first time. When a new member joins, she may be unable to speak her own name. She has been so timid and self-effacing, she will cover her mouth when she talks.' One third of SEWA members are rural women, a third are Muslim, a third Untouchables.

Ela Bhatt believes that the international labour move-ment must be flexible enough to include women and the self-employed, and not see itself only in terms of mono-lithic blocks confronting big employers. Women can show other forms of solidarity.

Late in the afternoon the bank is crowded. Women are working in the shaded courtyard, ink-block printing on cotton fabrics, doing agarbatti and cane work, finding there a more ample space than in the crowded huts. SEWA is a vital and creative place, a practical demonstration of the energy and power of women. It speaks to the experi-ence of women everywhere, invites the cementing of soli-darities across barriers of race, religion and continent.

Connections

The relationship between the rich and poor of the earth has only been made more explicit through those who have migrated into the labour market of Western Europe and North America. Those connections are clear enough. But with an increasingly integrated single world market, and the new international division of labour, so many objects of daily use and consumption come from parts of the globe formerly distant. The ties that bind our lives ever more closely to people who are ill-paid, and exploited are often the object of great concealment. Indeed, the activities of busy publicity, advertising and marketing industries serve to illuminate all the things that are on sale in the West in a pure light of desirability, eliminating the pain and exploitation that went into their creation.

Christmas 1987

It is especially at Christmas time that the vaunted superi-ority of the Western way of life is most in evidence. For then, the shops are full of the most variegated merchan-dise, the most fabulous abundance. The images speak for themselves, and to the whole world; a source of fascination to those limited by the functional austerities of the socialist countries, a compelling motive to those energetic migrants from the Third World to find a way somehow to reach the glittering metropolis.

And yet, how omnipresent is that Third World, in the objects and artefacts on display! The bazaars of the West evoke the invisible labour of the entire globe, even though all traces of it have been eliminated from the dressed windows, with their ghost-white Christmas trees hung with scarlet and gold, their rivers of silver tinsel, their stylized models of inimitable perfection, their festoons of metallic garlands, their false evergreens. The unseen presence is there, if only in the labels that name the country of origin of the manufactured goods.

An hour in any shopping centre in Britain is like a breathless tour of the world: a hint of the single global market of which we form an irretrievable part. There are shirts on sale from Mauritius, jeans from the Ivory Coast. Is it possible not to wonder whose fingers sewed them? Under what conditions and for whom are they produced? Is it the whisper of the tissue paper that suggests the sigh of the woman working late into the night, while her children sleep — where? — on fibre mats, on an earth floor, under the night sky? Are those flecks of blood or simply faults in the plastic of the Christmas trees made in Taiwan, and sold for a mere £3.99 apiece? These, for sure, will be mass produced in factories. What rights do the workers have? Is the work seasonal, or do they make Christmas trees all the year round for the — mainly — poor of the rich world? The trees are flame-retardant: on whose insistence was this safety feature incorporated; and what would halt the flames should fire break out where the workers live? And what do we know of those who labour in the South Korean factory that produces the terrarium, hand-made and of glass, such an attractive container for our exotic house-plants? What is their purchasing power over the necessities of life when they have done furnishing us with these interesting articles? It is easier to pass quickly to the luxury accessory packs for the wrapping of gifts. These are made in the USA, where working people, surely, do not labour under the same disadvantages of their unrecognised kin in South-East Asia. It is difficult not to wonder why we add to our balance of payments difficulties by importing these objects — fancy shapes and stars of ribbon that you stick on gifts; perhaps it is to help the even graver American trade deficit.

In any case, this year, most shops are offering a gift-wrapping service, to save us all that tiresome hard labour on Christmas Eve, with flimsy paper and coloured string. Much of this useful material has come from Hong Kong, a valuable source of employment which will surely not be interrupted after 1997 when it reverts to China. Indeed, China itself also seems to have learned a thing or two: its exports are on prominent display. The bamboo baskets in which the Body Shop is offering its presentation packs stand in great cardboard containers direct from the People's Republic. That country has also supplied Woolworth's with some artificial holly and some fantasy porcelain figures.

Nor have the workers of South Korea been neglecting the great Christian festival of the West: they have been manufacturing capacious red Christmas stockings, in which countless delighted children will be rummaging in the early hours of December 25th. If maintaining the legend of Father Christmas is nice for the children, the legends that sustain adults are even more essential: without them, they might be tempted to wonder under what circumstances these greedy containers for their offerings to their young have come into existence in the world.

Similarly with the Taiwanese outdoor lights that are being tastefully looped around the dark evergreens in front gardens and driveways all over the suburbs, shimmering magically in the mist. Of course, there are some products whose origin defies all efforts to trace them. Where, for instance, are Dreamland International toys created? It seems an appropriate metaphor for the slums and shanties and sweat-shops from which so many good things are wondrously wafted to us across the oceans, to appear, cleaned and candid before those who have the money to spend.

The Care Bears are clearly labelled Taiwan. They say Touch Me on the red heart embroidered on their paw; and when you do, they sing in a disembodied voice an electronic carol, an eerie, unearthly lullaby to soothe the anxieties of adults. The dream-glow tutu of the Barbie doll has come from the Philippines (although the parent corporation in the USA does not disdain to fix its own logo to the label.) Barbie is no longer alone. She is accompanied now by Ken, also from Manila, and his clothes, too, are luminous.

A stall is selling real leather photograph albums for instant Christmas snaps, once again provided by the compliant workers of South Korea, who are doubtless eagerly anticipating the spending of their surplus wages on mementoes from the 1988 Olympics, if their huts have not been demolished in the interests of beautifying Seoul so as not to offend the susceptibilities of all the rich visitors. India has contributed some of the most sublime silk blouses, miraculously sheer, and hand-sewn with hundreds of sequins. The brilliance of them makes the eyes water, although perhaps not quite as much as the eyes of the women who made them, huddled in the most squalid hutments of the city of Ahmedabad, and working for the merest fraction of the money the middleman got, or the wholesaler, or the exporter, or the importer; beautiful objects which increase in value by no more remarkable a process than their effortless movement across the continents.

It is with some relief that we return to more functional products — some food for a special accompaniment to the Christmas meal. A little mange-tout from Guatemala, some baby-corn from Thailand, some succulent Brazilian mangoes to clear the palate, a handful of preternaturally red cherries from Chile. Economics readily explains why poor countries grow luxury fruits and vegetables for export: it is so that they may earn the foreign exchange that will permit them to buy back the staple food that the people once grew for themselves.

So, to the Body Shop, with its natural products and its announced attachment to Friends of the Earth; there to buy some strawberry body shampoo, some jojoba and wheatgerm with nutmeg oil, or some camomile, geranium and royal jelly moisturiser, or coconut oil lotion. The plundering of natural resources in order that the rich of the earth should be able to wallow in what seem to be largely foodstuffs may appear a curious form of dedication to conservation. Who, we may wonder, harvests the nutmeg, who owns the copra plantations? Do the workers climb the palms barefoot under the hot sun, and do they never fall to their death from the fragile branches chattering in the tropical wind?

Perhaps it is best to stick with manufacturers from those countries where the people are known to be free. The USA is well-represented, especially in the provision of some of the most sophisticated toys. The model remote-control Bell Huey helicopter is on sale for some deserving youngster at £699.99. For the less affluent, why not a .357 Magnum 4in. barrel gun, the perfect Smith and Wesson replica, the M16 pump-action? Or a Manta Force game: a multiple air, naval and terrain assault force. Naturally, the Masters of the Universe is conspicuously marked USA. Even in toys, it seems, the arms trade is a major feature of American exports.

Japan has cornered the market in electronic toys: there is a walkie-talkie to help your children conduct their fantasy battles with greater efficiency. The transformers are also from Japan: Grax who changes into Skullcrusher's Head.

In the end, of course, we all want things that endure; and what looks as good as it feels, according to the ads on the bus shelters, if not gold? How good it feels to the producers is scarcely any concern of ours; their high fatality rate in the goldfields of South Africa, their barrack housing, their separation from their families melt into air when confronted by the beauties into which the results of their labour are wrought: the charms for bracelets of Big Ben or dancing shoes or a horn of life, or the setting for a tiger's eye ring or some opal ear-studs, or, this year's special pledge to the future, baby-bangles in pure gold.

This then is the true magic of the markets. The blood and filth and pain that attend the creation and origin of these wonders are miraculously washed away by the money that can afford to buy them. If the Western system has delivered the goods to the people, as it claims, it has also delivered the people, the poor of the earth, bound hand and foot, to the goods.

The role of the salespeople and advertisers in obscuring these connections cannot be overstated. One of the most extraordinary by-products of the information-rich societies is the creation of a kind of unknowing, even ignorance, that is strangely at odds with the profuse means of communication that they have at their command. Indeed, some observers have seen in this process a human-made replica of older patterns of natural ignorance, whereby people today have become as unaware of the origin, the violence, the exploitation involved in the production of everyday articles and necessities as the peas-antry was once unaware of the forces that governed the rhythm of lives in bondage to the vagaries of the seasons and to the owners of the earth they cultivated. A new and artificial techno-peasantry is in the making: it is to this version of pauperizing people in the rich countries that the advertising industry is dedicated.

The role of advertising is less that of hidden persuader than its critics maintain. Its principal contribution to our civilization is that it serves the one-sided and partial account of human possibilities promoted by rich Western societies in what William Leiss has called 'a culture of wanting.' Its purpose is to legitimize all wants, without hierarchies or distinctions, so that whim, caprice, desire, yearning and need become indistinguishable. The advertising industry is the forge in which human desire is melted down and recast in the image of capitalist necessity. It is clear that we are here in the presence of something awesome and numinous — the religious art of a throwaway age. The cumulative effects of advertising display people in postures of sustained ecstasy: an iconography of transfiguration. The uniform desirability of everything leads to a morbid desire for the unattainable: to acquire everything we want would take all the money in the world, that secular substitute for divine grace.

Of course, advertising is only the visible presence of purchasing power, the word made flesh as it were. To abstract it from a system of which it is only an expression is unfair. But it remains one of the most significant conduits of the values we live by, because of the way in which it concentrates on the moment of communion between human being, money and product, that unacknowledged profane trinity. The instant of buying is the most intense and concentrated experience that our culture offers to the individual.

The explosive and blinding light that transfigures the moment of communion creates all around it a vast area of darkness and confusion. Its effect is to obliterate all concern for the origin of the product and for the possible consequences of the transaction. A nimbus of unknowing clouds the provenance of the article or symbol purchased. The moment of buying has been sanctified, bathed in a purifying refulgence. All the rest is consigned to the unknown and the unknowable: the things we can afford are thus sundered from all antecedents, all unpleasant associations.

The separation of consumers from producers has been one of the greatest triumphs of the global capitalist market. This development has been made easier by the suppression of much manufacturing industry in the rich Western countries, which estranges the people from the kind of knowledge that comes only from direct experience of seeing the rich and powerful profit from your skills and labour. The deindustrialisation of Britain has been accompanied by a loss both of consciousness and memory.

The legitimation of all wants and their undifferentiated equivalence in the presence of money has profound implications. For instance, the famous freedom of choice, which is supposed to be one of the distinguishing marks of our civilization, is undermined by the erasure of understanding of where so many objects, artefacts and items of consumption that are the focus of that freedom come from. The elision of the pain and sacrifice involved in their mysterious and dazzling appearance in the assembly of commodities allows us to live in collusive dissociation from the consequences of our wants.

Freedom of choice, what the people want, sounds like a rallying-cry, one of the few sure clarion-calls in an uncertain world. But if those choices are made in a vacuum, where ignorance of the origins of what we buy is matched only by heedlessness of the implications for the destiny of others in each purpose, then the absolute quality claimed for such freedoms is seriously impaired. To be more precise, if we do not know who has suffered in the production of the most trivial commodities, how can we judge what our choices mean? And if we cannot — or will not — judge, how can they be free choices at all?

The indifference towards who else really pays, and in what coin, under what circumstances of life, on whose terms, actually invalidates the cherished notions of adults freely choosing, for it shrouds in unknowing real living relationships. It becomes more like the sheltered world of certain versions of childhood, into which any knowledge of sin or death may not enter. The well-regulated promotion of certain kinds of ignorance is the commodity for which many talented and creative people are paid so extravagantly in our society. Theirs are rituals of purification; and they are rewarded as befits their priestly caste. The multiple impoverishments that derive from the whole process — for producers and consumers alike — are at

the root of the patterns of maldevelopment that disfigure
the rich and poor countries alike.

Inside Asia's largest slum

Of course we are far from the establishment of a truly
integrated world market; for that would mean that every
region of the earth would be pitted against every other
one in competition for work. Those who have protested
that certain enclaves of Britain are more like the Third
World than the 'developed' West (cardboard city, for
instance in central London, some of the derelict estates
and crumbling inner-city areas) miss the point: this is only
the beginning of 'integration.' The question is not whether
parts of Britain and the West should be preserved from
becoming like the Third World, but whether the people
of both North and South have the will to fight for their
own joint liberation from the processes which set them
against each other in the first place. Failure will result in
more places like Dharavi making their appearance, not
only in the cities of the South, but elsewhere in the world
also.

Although Dharavi doesn't appear on the official map of
Bombay, it has long been known as the largest slum in
Asia. To those who live there, it is known as the 'langoti'
or loincloth of Bombay: it covers the private parts, the
places visitors don't see. But if it is Bombay's shame, it is
also a source of great energy and vitality.

It covers 420 acres. When the settlement began in the
mid-1930s, it was beyond the city limits, a swampy dumping-ground for garbage and unwanted squatters on the
sidewalks of the great imperial city. A government of
Mahrashtra survey last year found 275 000 inhabitants,
but a people's census, conducted by the Slum-dwellers'
Federation of India, produced a figure of 680 000. They
admit a margin of error up to twenty per cent, but this
still means a figure close to half a million people.

The largest single group are from the South of India,

Tamil Nadu. Landless, victims of caste and communal violence, they make up thirty-seven per cent of the total. Those from Maharashtra of which Bombay is the state capital — make up thirty-four per cent: many of these are neo-Buddhists, converted from Untouchability by Dr Ambedkar in the 1950s. The census also identified about 80 000 men living in 'pongal' houses, sleeping in bunks in shifts throughout the day and night — just as occurred widely in the cities of Britain in the early industrial period. Dharavi is like an extensive refugee camp, of people fleeing drought, dispossession and oppression. The crooked maze of passages separating the tin huts is so dense that only the narrowest slivers of sunlight reach the earth. Some of the buildings have expanded upwards, substantial structures of brick with tiled floors, but most are of rusting frayed tin, roofs covered with hessian, tarpaulin, polythene, anything that will mitigate the fierce heat of the sun in this barren, shadowless place.

Work is the most conspicuous reason for the existence of Dharavi; the work of women is the most visible, making papad and bidis on the threshold of the houses, selling tomatoes, aubergines or crimson onions, cooking on small fires at the edge of the channels of waste water, working on garments for export at sewing machines, or beating the dirt out of their washing by striking it against smooth stone slabs.

Dharavi is a city within a city. You can buy anything here, from paan and cigarettes, bicycles and watches, to shirts and biscuits. You can buy an airline ticket to London or hire a bullock-cart. You can buy gold, either smuggled or on the open market; you can see movies in a cinema or in production. There are prostitutes available for one rupee or a thousand rupees. Goods produced in Dharavi are on sale all over the world.

And those goods emerge from the most squalid places. Much of the tanning and leather work of Bombay is carried out here. Sheds of rough brick with tin roofs through which the burning presence of the sun can be felt;

dirt floors running with blood and shreds of flesh scraped from the animal skins that come straight from the abattoirs. The skins soak in deep square pits, and are fished out of the ochre-coloured chemicals with a long pole; they are then slung over a board where men pare away the animal remains which simmer in a feral stench. Men who have been working here for twenty-five years earn 25 Rupees a day (a little over £1). Many of the workers are stunted and disabled from polio or malnutrition, many of them Untouchables. A boy of twelve abandoned by his mother when his father died, works from eight till five cutting leather into strips for 7 Rupees a day. (about 35p). Close by is a foundry, where aluminium bases for office swivel-chairs are smelted and cast. A vat of alloy bubbles in a square brick furnace, the coals white-hot; the aluminium seethes, the crust bursts from time to time, emitting a strong silver light. The men here wear nothing but shorts, and their bodies run with sweat. They are all from Tamil Nadu; a man of twenty-five can earn 35 Rupees a day, but within ten years his working life will be over. The atmosphere is saturated with coal-dust, ash and particles of metal.

The few open spaces in the slum are full of offal and waste — melon-rind, banana skins, straw, paper cut-offs, rags, cigarette packets, egg shells form a small mountain of garbage, across which children work methodically, collecting anything that can be recycled. Through the middle of the slum runs a canal, an almost motionless stretch of turbid paste-like liquid. Almost waist-high in this substance a dark boy of about eleven struggles, diving into the indigo dyes and excreta to bring out pieces of glass, plastic containers, battered chappals.

Just as you think you have seen the worst that even Dharavi can offer, you come across a bone-crushing factory, a fish-meal works, yet another skin-processing shed. A group of workers from Bihar work barefoot in an unlighted unventilated hangar, cleaning freshly skinned bullock hides and preserving them in salt. They stand ankle-deep in foul-smelling gelatinous flesh, working soundlessly, the only noise coming from the sharp knives rasping against the skins in such a way that no flaw will appear on the finished article. They work ten months a year, six days a week; at harvest time they return to Bihar to help their families on the small plot of land.

There are also many things of great beauty produced in Dharavi. One carefully concealed factory buys dried peepul leaves from the tribal people who desiccate them so that they are like fabric, and the workers print silk-screen designs onto then. Each leaf is then painted by girls sitting round a long table: every girl uses just one colour to add a single detail to the tiny landscape or face that has been printed on the leaf. This factory has no licence, pays no taxes. All the leaves are exported to Europe and the USA. The girls are paid 15 Rupees a day. The owner — a former painter of signs — gets 5 Rupees for each leaf, but they are eventually sold for up to ten times as much. Not only goods are exported, but people too. Every flight to the Gulf disgorges a sad frieze of young women to work as domestic servants. Women like Fatima, for instance, a handsome, powerful woman who came to Bombay from Tamil Nadu. She had six children, but three died in infancy. Her husband drank, and in order to punish him she went to Qatar to work as a servant. With her employer, she travelled to Mecca, to Singapore and to London, where she spent two months without ever going outside. Her husband died of drink and she came home; her thirteen-year-old works in a factory making leather handbags.

Recently, the future of Dharavi has become a subject of great interest to others than its inhabitants. Two year ago, Rajiv Gandhi announced that 10 crores of Rupees (about £50 million) would be spent on upgrading slums; about 370 million would go on Dharavi alone. The truth is that this once-remote ex-urban settlement has become the very centre of Bombay, and a coveted piece of real-estate in a city where land prices rival those of London or New York.

The builders and developers can scarcely contain their excitement. This marshy, low-lying wasteland, which the slum-dwellers themselves have filled in and raised against the floods for half a century, is now far too valuable for them to be permitted to remain there. The Prime Minister's Grand Plan is to provide 'affordable housing': this means apartments, mainly for the middle class and far beyond the reach of the majority of people living in Dharavi: the cheapest flat in the new plan would cost about 30 000 Rupees. There is enough wealth in the slum for about a quarter of the people to be able to afford such accommodation, according to Mr Gnanamuthu, Secretary of the Society for Community Organisation of Urban Poor (SCOUP). For most people, the plan will mean displacement and dispersal. The discrepancy between the official count of the population and the real numbers is measure of the removals that would occur: the development plan allows for only 55 000 families to be rehoused on the site.

SCOUP and the Slum-dwellers' Federation have begun a campaign for a different kind of development, where the people themselves would become the owners of the land they occupy, and would upgrade and improve their own dwellings. Otherwise, the people who will be displaced will simply move further North, into the next area of marshland and insalubrious mangrove swamp. There, they will create another vast slum. After twenty years, when the land has been filled in and improved, it too will become valuable, and the construction industry will try to get its hands on it for yet more apartments for the rich.

Geeta Naik came to the haven of anonymity of Dharavi in 1972, after a marriage of which her Goan family disapproved. She has been working to organize the people in her particular slum (one of sixty-two separate 'nagars' or communities within Dharavi), to demand that the land they occupy be given to the people on a community basis. At least twenty-one co-operative societies have been formed in the slum with this end in view, and bank accounts have been opened, many of them in the names of the women, who are the real builders and home-makers. The government has been obstructing the registration of these co-operative societies. Geeta Naik says 'The people themselves can do the work to upgrade the slum. Of the 370 million Rupees for Dharavi, they've already spent a quarter on American town planning consultants, an architect from London, experts, planners, professionals. The people can build their own homes, why should they be depowered by professionals? There is a big project, costing 4 million Rupees, the Mithi River cleaning project. It would take the people of Dharavi one day's labour to do it for nothing. We have the qualifications, we are the experts — we've lived here for most of our lives.'

The government is watching us, says Mr Subramanian of the community organization. 'They want to see how far we can mobilize public opinion for our plan. They are afraid of us, because they've come to believe their own propaganda — they want the world to think that Dharavi is full of thieves and goondas. The great majority of us are hard-working people who don't want to lose control over our lives.'

Of course Dharavi has the same social problems of any poor area — drugs are increasingly available to the poor in Bombay; and many of the unemployed young men spend their time watching pirated blue movies from the West. There is a liquor problem, illicit stills making arrack, which is sometimes adulterated with chemicals. 'But the real social problems are the corruption of the police, the politicians and protection rackets. They can't bear that we should own our own piece of land, because we would then become independent of the slum-lords and the strong-arm men and the politicians; not to mention all the other managers of exploitation — the planners, the animators and the social workers, the manipulators of human souls. We came to this place as a wasteland. We made it home.'

CHAPTER FOUR

Pauperizing people

The pauperizing of people in Dharavi, their subordination to experts, the confiscation of their skills, the disgracing of their capacity to build their own homes, has its parallel in the way the people of the West have become pauperized even while apparently enjoying an increase in their standard of living. The ways in which human beings become poor are many and subtle. As E.P. Thompson points out, in *The Making of the English Working Class,* 'it is possible for people to become richer and less free at the same time'; and Rudolf Bahro, in *Socialism and Survival,* says that the people of Western Europe were awarded the Welfare State after the Second World War, as a consolation for their lost liberties. Impoverishment means not only a decline in monetary income; it can also mean the loss of skills, the decay of respect, the erosion of a sense of function or purpose, the disgracing of traditional forms of wisdom. All the celebrated and much-trumpeted gains that have been made by the people of the West amount to little more than trifling sums of money; and these have been accompanied by epic forfeits — power and control over our lives, the atrophy of skills and abilities, the loss even of the memory of how to do things for ourselves, installed as we are, in the most terrifying dependency of all — the abject and inescapable dependency upon money and what it will buy.

Nowhere is this undermining of people's faith in themselves and traditional wisdom more glaring than in the reduced role and decayed function of the old.

The view from the geriatric ward

The building was the town workhouse, which for a hundred years cast its shadow over the lives of the people in the adjacent streets. Its dark red bulk is now dissimulated behind a painted two-storey facade, its long wards are partitioned by curtains and hardboard; but the menacing memory of its past function remains with many of the patients in what is now a geriatric hospital. Perhaps it is a reaction to the idea of 'workhouse' that makes so many of the old people complain of an extreme absence of any occupation. They don't even have a daily newspaper. They are dying, as one old woman said, of boredom.

There are twenty women in the ward. Perhaps half of them are bed-bound. The dayroom for the less disabled is an addition to the building; so narrow that the half dozen who use it must sit in a row in the leather chairs. There is a green carpet, wallpaper with a pattern of silver and green leaves; the white radiators are warm against the chill August afternoon. Princess Diana smiles down shyly. In the corner, a television plays, at such an oblique angle to the chairs that no one can see it without craning uncomfortably: it talks to itself, almost like one of the residents.

A programme about antiques is showing: a woman has brought a goblet to be valued: when she learns it is worth eight or ten thousand, she is overcome with emotion and has to be led away in tears.

The visitors tend to spend most of their time talking to each other; the television mutes the anxieties and tensions, and covers the silences, and the awkward moments when the old women address dead husbands or absent children. They have all been neatly dressed, their hair done with coloured plastic clips to keep it in place; the whiskers have been removed from their chins. Ranging from their late 70s to early 90s, some are confused; others have moments of piercing clarity.

The picture windows of the annexe look out onto the gardens — Peace and Danse du feu roses, battered after the storms, their petals scattered. The wind shakes the rain in silver beads from the spiky branches of the shrubs. The gardener is going to lose his job as part of the present cost-cutting drive.

The Sunday afternoon is long. Dinner was over by quarter past twelve, and was, they all agree, scarcely edible: the carrots were hard, the potatoes weren't cooked, the meat stringy; one of the few enjoyments of the very old spoiled. Every time the door opens, the heads turn together. The rest of the time, they talk desultorily, offering up the bare bones of their lives, starkly, reduced, just as they are, as they sit emaciated and immobile. 'Silly boy, he went and died on me on Christmas Eve, after 46 years. He always used to say "I'll see you all right; but how can I be all right without him?" '

'My first husband was no good. He used to hit me. I'd say "What was that for?" " — Because I felt like it." Whenever he came home, I had to take the kids and lock myself in the attic. Then my second husband, he was lovely. Only he went and set fire to himself in the armchair.'

'My husband was a skilled man. He always worked. He tipped up his wage-packet on the kitchen table every week.' It is unbearably poignant to hear the old women define themselves in terms of their men: wraiths defined by a shadows.

'I don't care what happens to me when I'm dead', says one woman, 'but I bloody well care what happens to me between now and then.'

The children do come, even if they don't stay long. They're on their way somewhere, they've left something cooking, they're baby-sitting. They offer comforting words that they think will make their parents' position easier to bear. 'It's a terrible day, more like October than August. You're in the best place here.' 'If this is the best place', says Connie fiercely, 'God help us when we get where we're going.'

The visitors talk to each other about their holidays: what a wonderful time they had in Greece, how friendly everyone was, how they loved Venice, how they've dreamed of retiring to Tenerife. The women have nothing to contribute to these conversations. Only later, they will express their disappointment. I wonder why my granddaughter didn't come. Of course my boy can't be running down here every five minutes. He works so hard, he doesn't have any time to himself. They have their own lives to lead. The reasons and rationalizations of a gentle disengagement: why aren't I a greater part of their lives which they are so busy leading?

Laura has had a leg amputated. She has to go back for more surgery in a few weeks' time. She is deaf and has cataracts on her eyes, but her sharp intelligence is unimpaired despite her handicaps. Unfortunately, no one recognizes this, and she is spoken to in that chivvying slightly exasperated tone that people use to those whose understanding is impaired. She says 'It's funny really, we've so much time on our hands, even though we have so little time left. We think we're killing time, but it's time that is killing us.'

Joyce has taken possession of the bag of sweets that somebody had brought to share round. 'Yes', she says to her son when he calls in for a brief visit, 'I had them given to me.' And she eats them all, one after the other; even though last night she had woken up with terrible pains in her chest, couldn't get her breath. They had sent for the doctor. Indigestion. Joyce used to live on the South Coast, but she came North to be close to her two sons. 'People aren't close, not like they used to be. You can't expect it. People are so busy. Busy doing what?'

Maria came from Italy years ago, and never learned English; her children learned to interpret for her. She sits at the end of the row of chairs, weeping. Laura tries to comfort her, a tone of voice, a stroking of the hand.

Maria's memory has failed, and she is locked in a permanent present. Although her daughter-in-law works in the hospital as an ancillary worker, she has gone to Italy for a fortnight's holiday with her family. Maria feels only their absence; for all she knows they will never return. Her rosary is tangled over her metal walking-frame. A compatriot, also an ancillary worker, brings her a peach, because she has stopped eating. The younger woman talks to her in Italian. 'She used to be a wonderful dressmaker, made clothes for all her family, wedding dresses too that would take your breath away.' Pinned up all round her bed are coloured cards with embossed gold messages saying 'Get Well Soon', 'Hope You Make a Speedy Recovery.'

Some of the visitors bring little treats — a nip of whisky, a lemon mousse in a scalloped plastic container, a home-made sandwich. 'What I'd really like is a nice piece of cake. I haven't had a decent piece of cake since I've been here.' 'You still moaning Joyce?' 'I'm not moaning. I don't mean to, but I suppose that's what it sounds like. I know they do their best.'

Soon after tea, a nurse comes in and says 'Anyone ready for bed?' One of the men visitors says 'Yes please'. Everybody laughs. The nurses on the day shift put to bed all those who want to go before seven, which is the great majority. This is because the night staff are agency nurses, who don't have the continuity or the commitment of the day staff, and they are correspondingly rougher and less thoughtful than the regular workers. The old people say they are frightened of them. The dayroom empties, until only Joyce is left, still munching sweets and watching a murder on television.

There are only two nurses to put twenty patients to bed. It is a slow process. One woman tries to get out of bed: her legs become entangled with the rails at the side. There are calls for nurse all over the ward. A woman is calling for her mother. A husband comes to see his wife: he is eighty-eight, and he asks her plaintively why she isn't coming home, why she has left him. She knows he can't fend for himself.

The late visitors leave. They agree that old age is a tragedy; and they seem to be moved by a strange sense of urgency that it is your duty to enjoy yourself while you can, not get caught out before dark having done nothing and been nowhere; and yet, the intensity of the old women's feelings as they recall their dead sisters, husbands, parents, suggests that their affections have been no less profound for having been place-bound, tied for long years to factory and home. They seem to reproach their young with something for which neither they, nor their children, are responsible. Here, you can feel like a physical pain the pressures applied to the deepest human relationships, the most loving associations. 'I love my mother, but I could never live with her. We don't have room. She wouldn't be happy.' 'I'm out at work all day, she's better off with people her own age.' 'I come as often as I can, but I couldn't look after her. She needs professional care.'

All the old women are in bed, and it is still daylight. The skies clear a little and some late sunshine makes a rainbow over the former workhouse.

Forgetting

The psychiatric hospital in the same town, with its red Byzantine tower, its long gravelled drive and evergreens, is now largely given over to the care of the confused elderly. Many of the patients are former workers in the town's sometime main industry, men and women who started work at thirteen or fourteen, whose workplaces and homes have long been demolished. Many of them are now suffering from Alzheimer's disease. Their relatives, distressed, and sometimes ashamed, that they can no longer look after them at home, have consented reluctantly to seeing them pass into the care of strangers. The old man who can no longer attend to his wife's needs because his own strength is failing, the individuals watching over those they have loved night and day, find the anxiety too hard to bear: the old woman is brought home after having been 'caught' in Boot's with her battered leather shopping bag full of shampoo, lipstick and eyeshadow; the grandfather who is found by a neighbour peeing in the gutter; the woman whose unassuaged resentments make her declare to her husband that she isn't married to him and never has been.

In one ward of the hospital, there are two sisters and a sister-in-law who lived in the same street all their lives. Although they saw each other almost every day for more than half a century, they no longer recognize one another. Cared for by strangers now, they have become strangers to one another. Forgetting by the elderly — that harrowing disintegration of identity, where knowledge decays, while feelings only seem to become more intense, with the result that people remain, hauntingly, themselves, and yet, at the same time, not quite themselves, tantalising shadows of those we knew, tearing at the heart-strings long after all other bonds have been broken — is a powerful metaphor for processes which, if not socially determined, have at least a strong social component. At the least, they are exacerbated by the discontinuities of rapid social change. In the testimony of those who have cared for relatives suffering in this way, there is a pattern: the desperate efforts to contain the disorder, to recall them to the forgotten sense of self. People who love them talk of the exasperation that can lead to them slapping the forgetting person into recognition; to locking the bedroom door, to putting a padlock on the fridge to prevent an old man from eating half a pound of butter or the cat food. One woman said that she bound the bedclothes so tightly around her mother's bed that she was virtually imprisoned by them, and was physically unable to get up and wander in the night. It sometimes appears to those who are watching over people afflicted that this dementia has a strong element of wilfulness. Bursts of guilt at their own impotence follow surges of unreasonable and desolating anger. It sometimes seems as if *they are doing it on purpose.*

And, at a deeper level, it is hard not to feel that they are indeed colluding, at a deeper level, only too readily with an erasure of memory of an awkward and unwelcome past. They are complying a little too eagerly with the shedding of a burden of experience which has, in any case, been consistently denied and rejected by the young for many years. They are only trying to help by their willingness to speed up that oblivion, that *social* forgetting of things which were, nevertheless, such a significant component of their identity. How often have they been told by their children and grandchildren in those repeated and circular family discussions 'Don't let us hear all that over again', or 'Times have changed', 'All that is over and done with', 'What's all that got to do with us?' whenever they have started on that litany of stories of hardship and poverty, how they considered themselves lucky as children if they were given the top of an egg, how they had picked up chocolate wrappings or orange peel in the street and kept it to get a savour of chocolate or oranges, the weekly visit to the pawnshop, the buckle-end of a father's strap that taught them right from wrong, leaving school at fourteen for a factory job and being sacked three years later to make way for younger, cheaper labour. All they could offer to those who came after was continuity, instruction, advice on how to deal with a poverty they had always known, but which seemed, suddenly, to their descendants, to have no place in their lives. For them, the air was full of promises of liberation: why should they listen to these memories of an experience become archaic and of no earthly practical use to their own expectations?

It is impossible to exaggerate the disturbance, the violence this produced in a generation grown to frugality, stoicism and want. It is not the smallest irony that now, when their wisdom and knowledge are most needed again in order to confront adequately the re-imposition of mass unemployment and poverty, their resourcefulness and understanding are no longer retrievable. The memories were not transmitted, but were expunged.

So when the years of the golden rule of money yield to a return to the time of its iron law, the young can face it only with the blankness of unfamiliarity. The descendants of those whose knowledge has fallen into decay are disarmed in the presence of the old inflictions. Poverty and unemployment appear to them new and strange in the altered setting in which they occur; for the memory of those things couldn't be suppressed quickly enough in the years of the mid-century when, it seemed, the times could only get better, and go on getting better for ever and ever.

In this way, it has a deeper meaning, that tendency for the old to decline towards the condition traditionally described as second childhood, and which seems to have been curiously aggravated in our time. Recognizing a transference of power, the old have striven to emulate those to whom their wisdom and authority have passed — to the very young, those for whom the old have no other characteristic than their often troublesome longevity. Perhaps it is by a process of unconscious imitation that the old try to retrieve something that they feel has been spirited away from them, falling almost unawares into the impotence of extreme infancy. While they themselves were still in their prime, their view of the future had set them at the centre of a group of listening grandchildren, who would eagerly absorb those carefully stored tales of triumph over adversity — how they had cheated poverty by making a meal out of next to nothing, with what art and skill they had deployed their always inadequate income, what moments of pleasure they had stolen in the narrow spaces between mill, chapel and workhouse.

Naturally, we are told by those who know, that senile dementia is abundantly researched, its origin well understood, its incidence increased by lengthened life-span, a private tragedy for thousands of families. But those who have lived to see the people we love reduced in this way

117

have another knowledge, a knowledge that has become inadmissible in these rich societies, because it cannot be sold for money, neither in the form of commodity or service, nor in the salaries of professionals. It is the knowledge that the estrangement of these old people is not simply an individual misfortune, but a process in which the social determinants are crucial, however unquantifiable. And however accurately it may be diagnosed or described, however lovingly treated by all the healers and restorers, there remains a dimension of the pain which they cannot reach.

And yet, it remains difficult to discover just how the young have been the beneficiaries of these processes.

Three generations

A house on a new estate on the edge of a new town; so extensive that it forms a self-contained township. It has a centre about half a mile away: a red plastic and smoky perspex structure visible across a landscape of grassed slopes, damaged saplings and a stream full of junk — bicycle wheels, mattresses, supermarket trolleys. The houses are terraced, set at angles to each other. They face a dual carriageway main road. There are paths at the back, with irregular patches of cotoneaster and Pyrocanthus, spiky shrubs to deter vandals and to catch crisp packets and sweet papers in their branches.

Three generations live in the house. The grandmother is thirty-eight, the mother fifteen and the baby two weeks old. The child is a beautiful girl with lots of hair, who weighed seven pounds nine ounces at birth. She sleeps in her plain box-shaped cot, her face pink against the white blanket, her arms outstretched. Grandmother says 'Put her bootees on'. 'She's warm as toast', the mother responds sharply, 'she's already got heat bumps from wearing too many clothes.' The older woman sighs. It is going to be hard for her not to interfere. She loves babies at this age;

just looking at the child makes her cry. 'It's the world she has got to grow up in.'

While the mother prepares the baby's feed, grandmother picks up the crying child. She holds her to her face, and the baby sucks vigorously at the woman's lower lip. She stops crying. By the time the mother comes in with the bottle, she is asleep again. Grandmother's lower lip is swollen. She says 'Now I've got bee-sting lips, very glamorous.'

The grandmother is a big woman. She has thyroid trouble. She wears a flowing pink floral-patterned dressing gown and fleecy slippers. 'I want to pick her up all the while. I love the smell of babies. Last night I looked after her. I gave her two feeds and took her into my bed.'

The mother has been unwell. She has had a kidney infection and now has a persistent cough. She hated being pregnant. Somebody told her she looked ugly, and she still feels it; although as she leans back on the sofa in her bright pink track suit, with the baby sprawled on her breast and stomach, she looks both attractive and more mature than she is. She shows some photographs of the child taken only six hours after birth, mounted on little cards, with details of the name, weight and time of arrival. In the space on the card where it says Parents, she has carefully deleted the 's' in biro before inserting just her own name.

She was frightened of giving birth. The pain lasted for fifty-one hours; the epidural was not completely effective. She had to be given a drug that delayed the labour in order to give her a few hours' sleep. She had sixteen stitches. The grandmother says, not without a certain satisfaction, 'She still hasn't got her figure back, she's got terrible stretch marks', as if to say, 'Now she knows what I went through'. At one time, the mother wanted me to write about her, in order to warn other young girls not to ruin their lives just because a bloke tells them one night he loves them. Now, she says, she feels quite different, and wouldn't be without the baby for all the world.

Grandmother says everything would be fine, 'unless they send me walkies next week.' She is to appear in court on five charges of fraud and deception. 'There were forty-one other t.i.c.s' She had taken a credit card and used it extravagantly on a two-day binge 'to get things needed for the baby. All the Social allowed us was £80. And for two weeks we had nothing at all. It's not as if I was stealing from people. Access, Barclaycard, they're not widows and orphans are they?' She had over a thousand pounds' worth of goods. 'My mistake was going into a restaurant with my mates. We had a big meal, spent too much, got greedy.' She says that if she ever gets another credit card — and it certainly won't be her own — on long-term social security that will never happen — she will know how to use it. 'Go into a shop, get what you want, then out, pronto. Don't hang around.' She says philosophically, 'We learn from our mistakes'; a piece of wisdom that refers, not to the morality of stealing a credit card, but to that of knowing how to use it without getting caught. If the case goes to Crown Court, she will almost certainly get a prison sentence.

'That's all we need.' The mother and baby would be left in the house with only a fourteen-year-old brother. She is right to feel worried. She says wistfully, 'But how else am I going to know what it's like to go into shops and buy things that other people take for granted? It's not my fault. I'm no worse than those who've made their fortune. Their money doesn't smell either, any more than mine did until I was found out.'

The fourteen-year-old comes in. He feels awkward and left out in the house of women. Laconic and macho, he moves in a way he has learned from older boys on the estate. He used to be a boxer, he explains, but his nose bleeds too easily. So now he practises martial arts, especially kung-fu. When asked how good he is, he says solemnly that he is not allowed to boast about his prowess. It is part of the art to be disciplined; you are expected to keep tight control of yourself at all times, even when you

120

are threatened; this skill is put to the test in self-defence. 'Otherwise you could kill too easy. But you have to be able to handle yourself in this world, look after yourself. I don't start fights. But if anybody tangles with me, they'll find out how good I am.'

The grandmother talks about her dissatisfactions with the neighbourhood. They had a lodger until recently, but she has gone: she is a Lesbian and has gone to live with a friend a few doors away. The husband of this friend is doing a long sentence in the nick. 'He was in the Hell's Angels. Before you can rise above a certain level, there are three tasks you have to do. One is to rob a grave, the other to commit a violent crime, I can't remember what the third is. Anyway, he beat up and raped this woman. And now he's trying to stir things up for his wife now she's living with another woman. He's saying the kids are being exposed to things they should be protected from. But he didn't mind when he was at home, while they were having threesomes and he used to watch the two women at it. What those kids saw then is worse than anything that's going on now. I'm worried about my friend, though. She's back on the drink since this husband is trying to get revenge. She scared that Social Services will take the kids away. She doesn't want to get the blame for that. While she was here, I got her off the drink completely.'

The phone was cut off last week. There was a bill for £107. A phone is a luxury for instant consumption — it lasts just until the first bill comes in. But she is worried that this means she has no contact with her own mother — baby's great-grandmother who is sixty — and who lives on the other side of town. She was widowed last year and a couple of weeks ago her next-door neighbour was murdered. 'What makes it worse is that the guy who has been charged was her neighbour on the other side. They were good neighbours to my mother. The bloke they killed was a nasty piece of work. He'd been playing loud music all summer long, day and night. My Mum had asked him to turn it down, and he'd told her to fuck off. This bloke had done four years inside for sex against children. So when my Mum's other neighbour goes to get him, he takes his son with him, boy of fourteen. They ask him to make less noise, and all they get is a load of lip. And he threatens to do to this fourteen-year-old what he'd been in the nick for. They went for him, knifed him. They only meant to teach him a lesson, only it got out of hand. My Mum is very upset. She's afraid of reprisals. She feels it's partly her fault — if she hadn't gone and asked him to turn down the music, none of this would've happened. She's already had some threatening phone calls.'

The grandmother is apprehensive about losing her freedom. It won't be the first time. She would like her life to be different — this wasn't how she planned it at all. 'I've never had anything. My husband beat me up before he pissed off, said he'd leave me something to remember him by. And now I'm fed up with living round here, going to the pub every day, seeing the same people, hearing them talk about the same things all the time. All they talk about is drugs and thieving and what was stolen yesterday and how much they got for it. I know I can tea-leaf, I'm not the world's greatest innocent, but at least I know there's other things in life. I like to have conversations that are a bit stimulating; what is life all about? Where are we going and why? Do you come back to earth again or is this it, is this all there is?'

The mother expresses her fears about the world that is waiting for her daughter. She is a serious and thoughtful young woman, worried about the threat of nuclear war and the poisoning of the environment. The grandmother too is anxious; only for her, it is poverty and insecurity that are the greatest threat, not being able to give the child the things she wants. Why should her flesh and blood go without?

More immediate threats seem to go unnoticed, although they're not unconnected: the depravity of the culture, the eclipse of moral values, the paramountcy of money. Yet the tenderness of the women, their love for each other and the hope invested in the child show that people remain, at one level, untouched by a harsh and degrading social climate. They know that they deserve better; yet the gulf between the personal feelings and the corruption of social values is a tension that surely cannot hold indefinitely; indeed, by next week, the grandmother may well be another statistic in the record number of the occupants of Britain's prisons.

As indeed she was. She served just over half of a six-month sentence. She had been out of prison for barely a fortnight when her house was wrecked. 'I had a big party when I came out, but even the best parties got to end.' While the grandmother was inside, her two children with the baby had stayed in the house, joined by a friend of the brother who had walked out on his parents a few doors away. During that time, the house was badly neglected. The young people had parties; they never cleared up after themselves. 'I asked my neighbour to keep an eye on them. She was as bad as they were. While I was away, the boys had been up in the roof. They bored holes in the ceiling so they could spy on whoever was in the bedroom and the bathroom. Nobody could do a thing in privacy, because the house had more holes than a bloody colander.'

Within a month of coming home, the grandmother lost her temper with the youngsters. She started on her daughter, but finished, as she always does, screaming at the boy. 'I don't know why, I just can't help it. Even when he hasn't done anything wrong, I go for him. I don't mean to. There's only one thing wrong with him, and that is that he'll grow up to be a bloody man.' She has always been badly treated by men. She likes her men young and glamorous. One of them used her while he was on parole, another got her to stand bail and then pissed off; her husband was screwing around while she was pregnant.

The young woman took her baby and walked out. She went to Social Services and they found her a place in a hostel for young mothers with children. 'It was her

123

sixteenth birthday last Saturday. I never phoned her, because last time I did, I just got an earful about being the worst mother in the last million years. Then she got mad because I never phoned her on her birthday. You can't win'.

The fourteen-year-old left to live with his father who has a flat in the city centre. 'He's always idolized his Dad, but it's easy to idolize somebody you don't live with. Once his Dad goes on one of his drinking binges, he might see he isn't Mr Wonderful.'

The grandmother says she doesn't really mind. At least her daughter has her own money now, and the boy will be his father's responsibility. This has left the grandmother with £11 a week since the child allowance money stopped; money is also being taken for rent, gas bills, debt. 'And as if that wasn't enough, somebody broke in one night when I'd gone out and wrecked the furniture. They tore the doors off their hinges, shit on the carpets, smashed up the beds. Nobody heard a thing. I don't know who it was, it could be anybody. Everybody round here has enemies. If it hadn't been for my neighbour taking me in, I'd've topped myself. She's a golden girl. I've had a bill for damages to the house. There's no way I can pay. I'm giving up the tenancy, go into bed and breakfast, start over. There's only one good thing about being at rock bottom — the only way to go is up.'

At the neighbour's house, her friends gather. They pool their experience as to what is best for the grandmother. Stay with your neighbour, bed and breakfast. Give up the house. Don't tell Social you're having full board. B & B you'll get £45 a week, plus personal allowances for meals and washing. If you go full-board, you'll only get £55 a week, all in. B & B you make an extra £15 a week.

The grandmother's acceptance of the separation from her daughter is made easier by the fact that it is becoming more advantageous for families to split up. 'You can't afford to live together. You split up, live separate. If the Social put the pressure on, get divorced. What difference does it make?' The grandmother says if something doesn't happen soon, it will be an overdose or back to crime. She says 'Thank God my daughter is all right. She's better off where she is, without me.'

A lot of people on the estate talk in this way. Of the separated husbands and runaway children and abandoned women, they say 'It's the best way. They have their own lives to lead.' A vocabulary of disengagement, withdrawal of people from each other; a fraying of the deepest bonds, fracturing of the closest relationships.

These fissures and breakings are not easy to measure; people don't always show them to a hostile outside world; but with one quarter of households in Britain now consisting of a single person, that doesn't make the unheard grief any less, or the pain easier to bear.

Chrissie's wedding

The day Chrissie had chosen for her wedding turned out to be bitterly cold. She had hesitated before marrying Kevin. It was, after all, her third marriage; and at twenty-seven, with four children under nine years old, she felt she had seen it all before.

This time, however, she is sure it will work. For one thing, Kevin is more keen than she is. This is the first time she has· entered a relationship in which she feels she has the emotional advantage. Kevin lived with her for a few months, but after a quarrel, he ran out, stole and crashed a car, for which he did six months.

While he was inside, Chrissie had begun to write to another man, also in prison. Later, she discovered that he had been convicted of sexual offences. Chrissie was told that if she invited this man into her home after his discharge from prison, the children would be placed on the at-risk register, and might well be taken into care. That settled it. Chrissie decided that a life with Kevin would be easier and more comfortable; especially since during the two and a half years she was on her own, her greatest pride was in having kept herself and the family together. She lived in dread of being called 'an unfit mother'. For her great courage and heroic efforts are not necessarily visible to the outside observer in any tangible achievement: the house is scruffy, the furniture wrecked, the walls defaced. Only those who really know her can have any idea of the pain and struggle that have gone into her precarious survival.

The marriage ceremony could not have been briefer. There were only the bride, the groom and two witnesses. Kevin came on the 8.58 a.m. bus into town; he couldn't afford a taxi. He was wearing a new suit in blue and pale grey check; his dark hair slicked down, his brown eyes scared. Chrissie got a lift in Michelle's car, which she had decorated with a white ribbon. As soon as she came into the Town Hall, she kicked off her shoes, which had already produced blisters. She wore a see-through blouse, pleated grey skirt, and she carried half a dozen orange roses. Michelle went to park the car, and was late for the ceremony. Chrissie became very anxious, because Michelle had the ring.

The registrar said 'Good morning all.' Under his breath, Kevin muttered 'He sounds like a copper.' Chrissie was told sternly to put her shoes on for the solemn event that was about to take place. In the room were twelve chairs with green leather seats; on a polished walnut table a slice of varnished wood and an arrangement of tiger lilies, and a dusty red cushion on which the ring was to be placed. On a side shelf there was a notice in a glass frame in Gothic script, which read 'According to the law of this country, marriage is a union between one man and one woman to the exclusion of all others.'

Afterwards, the certificate is given to Chrissie. 'Third time lucky', she murmurs. We are out of the Town Hall within six minutes of having entered it. As we come out into the November morning, the snow is falling gently. Chrissie says, with her good-natured smile, 'God's confetti.' They couldn't have afforded any other sort anyway.

We arrive back at the house before we are expected. The downstairs room has been tidied up, but Cindy is still hoovering. Kevin refuses to carry Chrissie over the threshold; she is much bigger than he is. There is a moment of sadness, because none of the parents could make it: it would have meant a long journey for Kevin's parents, and Chrissie's Mum couldn't get the day off work. However, the newly-installed telephone is much in use as they call up all those who couldn't be present to tell them the good news.

Cindy has done the catering: the table is full of ham, cheese and tomato sandwiches; squares of cheese on cocktail sticks, Bejam sausage-rolls, cup cakes, and a big square wedding cake iced in white, yellow and orange. On the sideboard there is a flagon of lager, a bottle of sherry, a bottle of Martini and a keg of bitter. The only other furniture is two burgundy-coloured chairs, with split fabric and foam gaping, and three yellow-painted kitchen chairs. A small black dog, which the children have given Kevin as a wedding present, dashes around the room, and jumps up at the food.

Chrissie's neighbours have been concerned to do things properly. A thin energetic woman called Freda, older than the others, takes charge, and as a kind of mistress of ceremonies gives instructions about the correct procedure. 'Toast first', she insists. Kevin pours sherry into the tumblers which Freda brought as her wedding gift. 'We'd be drinking out of mugs else' he says. Then the best man says a few words, and reads out the rhymes on the cards. On hers, Cindy has written: 'The three rings of marriage — first year engagement ring, second year wedding ring, third year suffering, ha ha.'

Michelle is glum. She has had a row with her boyfriend this morning and has to go back to face him. He moved in with her and the kids some months ago, and now he refuses to leave. 'Tell him it's your own wedding you've

127

just been to.' 'I would if I could get somebody six-foot four, built like a bus and a champion boxer. He broke the collar bone of the woman he was living with before me.' As Michelle goes, more friends arrive: Steve and Jenny, themselves married only a month ago. Jenny's little girl is five days old. There is a confused tangle of kinship in most of the families: bonds so fragile, it seems, they break at the slightest strain, leaving children to re-orientate themselves in new configurations of brothers and sisters and fathers and aunties. Indeed, parents often use their children as a means of divination: that they called Kevin 'Daddy' clinched Chrissie's decision to marry him.

Col, Freda's husband, has brought some neat industrial alcohol in miniature containers of Drambuie and Cointreau, and a bottle of his home-brewed elderberry wine, similarly fortified; a welcome means of eking out the drink. Col has grey hair in a 1950s style, and looks a little like an elderly Elvis. He and Freda have been married for six years; they lived together six years before that. 'You should always have your honeymoon first' says Freda. Cindy says that her mate had to go and pick two witnesses for her wedding from a bus queue outside the Registry Office. 'Witnesses, it sounds like an accident.' 'Mine was, I done myself a serious injury when I married him.' Freda organized Chrissie and Kevin to cut the cake. 'His hand on top of yours', she says severely. Kevin places a hand on Chrissie's breast. 'Put your hand over it.' Kevin covers his crotch. 'Come on', says Freda, 'let's have some music. I love dancing. I can go on all night, run rings round the youngsters. Let's get at the rock 'n' roll.'

There is a knock at the door. It is Pete, Chrissie's second husband, father of the two younger children. Chrissie knew he was coming. Indeed, there was something provocative in the invitation. He has brought Marie, his new girlfriend; they are to be married in the spring. Marie says she loves kids. 'Mine died', she says sadly. 'My baby had a hole in the heart and only lived ten minutes.' She wants children with Pete. 'Huh, wonder if he's told her he had a vasectomy' says Chrissie to Cindy. Marie and Pete linger in the kitchen. The tension rises. 'Aren't you going to offer us a drink?' Chrissie hesitates. 'I'll have to ask Kevin. He's the master of the house now. Kevin tells them to make themselves at home. Pete has changed his image: suit with waistcoat, series of gold studs in his ear, corn-coloured hair. He is now known as Vincent Colby — a tribute to Dynasty, and an assertion that his aspirations have risen since he was married to Chrissie. Pete and Marie talk loudly about starting their own business. 'You need something to leave your children, something to be remembered by.'

Another knock at the door. This time it is Janice and her friend Danny, both in motor-cycle gear: torn oily jeans, leather jacket dotted with silver spikes and death's head transfers. Danny says 'I apologise for the dress.' 'You're not wearing a dress, you're wearing jeans.' Janice says she didn't know there was a wedding on. She just called to see her mate Chrissie. 'Well, I had heard, only I didn't believe it. I couldn't believe you wouldn't invite me.' 'No', says Chrissie, 'we were going to bring a bottle round to you tonight.' 'The years we've known each other', says Janice, incredulous. 'I can't get over it.'

As the afternoon advances, the room becomes more untidy. The remains of children's sandwiches litter the floor, the puppy licks the cake-plates and crumbs of icing. The arrival of Pete, and then of Janice, gives an edge to the occasion that was in danger of being too bland. The disruption was foreseen, written into a scenario that suffered from an absence of passion. Chrissie's youngest child dirties himself. 'Go to Daddy', and the little boy makes for Kevin. 'Hey', says Pete, 'may I remind you that I am his father?' 'And may I remind you that Kevin is now married to me', says Chrissie.

'Kev is with the kids all the time.' Pete says that he hasn't yet given up hope of getting custody of the children. 'What kind of a life are they going to have with you, no ambition but living on the Social?' 'You're on the Social as well.' 'Not for long. Not when we get our business going.' Somebody puts 'Shotgun Wedding' on the record-player. Chrissie is very angry. 'That's one song I don't want to hear.' But the storm doesn't break until Janice, quite drunk, says 'I know why you didn't invite me. Kevin wanted me really, he was always asking me to go to bed with him.' Kevin denies it; he swears that Chrissie is the only one he ever wanted. There is a fight; tears and recriminations and declarations of revenge. 'Janice is always like that', says Cindy, 'she has to believe she's the one all the blokes want, she can't help it.'

It is nine o' clock. The reception has been going on for ten hours. Kevin and Chrissie are exhausted. They sink into a chair, make some coffee. The children are in bed. 'Thank God it's over', he says. 'Over, it's just starting.'

Next day Janice comes round. She has completely forgotten what took place; indeed, has no recollection at all. 'When I'm pissed I can't answer for anything.' Chrissie says 'Oh that's all right. It was a nice day.' 'Pity there weren't any pictures' says Kevin. 'And I'd've liked a honeymoon.' 'Never mind', Chrissie comforts him, 'we've got our memories. Something to look back on.'

Within six weeks Kevin had left home. He took and drove a car and crashed it again, and was soon in prison. Chrissie accused Janice of not giving her marriage a chance, but trying to take Kevin away from her. 'Just like Jolene in the song. She didn't want him, she just wanted to prove she could take him away from me.' Furious, Janice and some of her mates broke into Chrissie's house one night and beat her up in front of the terrified children. Chrissie left town, and went to live in a city some thirty miles away. When Kevin came out, he went to live with Janice and her new boyfriend. Within twelve months he was dating Chrissie's friend Cindy. After the divorce, Kevin and Cindy were married. Within a few weeks, he had run away from her. Janice said she thought Kevin wasn't sure whether he was gay or straight. 'He leaves his women and goes back to this bloke. Then he wrecks a car and goes into nick to sort himself out. Except he comes out in a worse state than ever. I did what I could for him. He needs help.'

Struggle for the soul of the poor

The poor of Labour iconography — worthy, serene in the expectation of a (deferred) millennium, patiently working for change in the party of hope — is as archaic as Victorian representations of the deserving poor. If we want to understand why Labour has, in general, failed to command the faith of the contemporary poor, we can do so only by looking at the life-style and values they aspire to. Because of their dependency upon the existing order, they are conservative and as deferential to the money they conspicuously lack as they might once have been to birth and breeding. Socialism is increasingly a foreign country, and its language unintelligible.

Paul and Lorraine live on an estate built in the 70s: a site of grassy slopes and beds of berberis and laurel. The houses are skimpily built with wire-reinforced glass doors and wide picture windows. They keep the curtains drawn all day, because, says Paul, 'You can't trust anyone round here.' He has two German shepherd-dogs, Sheba and Sabre. They are for protection. Paul controls them with a low whistle, but if anyone else goes near them 'they'll go for his throat.' In addition to the dogs, there is a chain and double lock on the door; as well as a Zulu spear on the wall, a samurai sword, and a Colt 45 under the table.

On the wall there is a Constable reproduction, a big card saying Happy Mother's Day, and a photograph of a woman's torso, just breasts and shoulders: she is taking off a flimsy sweater, revealing one naked breast, the nipple of which is painted so that it looks like the centre of a flower.

This is the best house Lorraine has ever lived in in her twenty-seven years. Since she has been with Paul, three years younger, she has stopped drinking. The money she would have spent has gone into the house, the carpets, the red plush three-piece suite. She waited for Paul the eighteen months he was in prison — her greatest triumph, and against the prediction of all her friends. Paul was convicted of armed robbery, for which he says he was framed. At the trial, he had jumped from the dock and escaped. He spent four nights in a foxhole outside the town. Despite police surveillance of the house, he went back, unseen. When the police came to the door, he hid in the dustbin. He had managed to prove his innocence of the armed robbery: at the very moment the crime was being committed, he had been arrested for speeding by the police of a neighbouring city. As a result, one policeman was dismissed and another demoted.

Paul is proud of his physical strength. He is small, five feet eight inches, wiry, energetic, very active. In spite of his lean frame, his chest measures forty-four inches and his biceps forty-four inches. In the nick, he spent his time body-building and weight-training. He prefers to fight with fists, because that gives him a sense of achievement; but if he is slighted, he will use any weapon to hand: he once cut off part of his brother's ear with an open razor, and he put someone through the glass of the front door. Even the police said to Lorraine with some admiration 'He's a fucking hard bastard.' He claims to feel neither cold nor pain. He has plastic kneecaps from a bike accident. His big Kawasaki stands on the trampled garden earth outside. Paul's father brought him up hard. 'And I mean hard. I wasn't six months old when he broke my arm. I was brought up to stand on my own two feet. Hit first and hit hard.'

'He can't show feelings', Lorraine says. 'He says he loves me, but when I say "Show it", he can't.'

'I've seen people hurt, not just physically, but mentally. I don't want that to happen to me . . . I don't know how to. I could never cry, not in front of anyone. No way. Not a man.'

One of the reasons why Lorraine has stuck with Paul is

that she is drawn precisely to his mastery of himself: what she has suffered from is absence of control. She was always being arrested for drunkenness, fighting, nicking things. She had had four children by the age of twenty-one; by nineteen, she had been married and divorced. She has cut her wrists, overdosed several times. But not since she has been with Paul.

Three of her children are now in care. Lorraine says 'I've got two choices; I can give permission for them to be adopted, or they'll be adopted anyway. I know I could look after them now. I've changed. They don't believe you can change.' She was sterilized, but since she has now been with Paul for three years, she now wants this reversed. 'I want him to say he'd like us to have a baby. Only he won't say it.' 'You've got to make the decision. If anything goes wrong, you'll blame me. You've got to do what you want.' Lorraine says 'See — he won't. I'd like to have all these tattoos on my arms taken off. If I had a baby and could get rid of these tattoos, I'd be happy. I don't think it's right for a kid to grow up with a mother covered in tattoos. It's not like a mother.'

Paul's lack of emotional display reminds her of her father. 'My mother stuck with him for years. He didn't really care for her; but she cared for him more than she did for me. She left him practically every week, but always went back. Then one day, she said she was going, waited till he'd gone to work, then took a taxi and went. The only thing my Dad loved was the drink. He's been given two years to live. His liver has been destroyed by it. One week, he drank sixty-eight bottles of sherry or VP wine. That's his breakfast, a bottle of sherry. I don't want to be like that.'

Paul and Lorraine feel they have settled down. Of course, it's relative. They are heavily in debt. Since they've been in the new house, they took out a loan of £150, and then a second loan. Now they owe £800. The gas is to be cut off next week for non-payment. Lorraine doesn't really mind. 'In the summer it's all right. I'll pay it off before next winter.' Although they don't drink, they occasionally smoke ganja. 'I wouldn't have anybody mainlining in my house', says Paul, 'but a smoke — it relaxes you. Late at night, you get involved in deep conversations about life and death.'

Lorraine believes in reincarnation. 'To me, you're born to die. If that was all, life wouldn't have any meaning. My Nan died the same day my youngest was born, almost at the same time. She was a lovely person, and I know her soul entered my child. I recognized her.'

Paul isn't frightened of death either. He enjoys bike scrambling, fast driving, the excitement of fighting. 'Live dangerous and die happy. There's no point in being careful. I could walk out of this house and slip on the pavement and smash my skull. If it's your time to die, there's nothing you can do about it. From the minute you're born, you've got an appointment with death, and you've got to keep it.'

Paul and Lorraine do not think of themselves as poor. They never have enough money, but that isn't the same thing. Their biggest complaint is the neighbourhood. 'The people round here, if they think you're happy, they'll try and split you up.' Or the mates who hang round all the weekend while there's food on the table and ciggies and a can of beer, then when it's their Giro day, they disappear without trace. 'And then, you can't let your kids out. There's a bloke round here been enticing kiddies out of the gardens where they're playing, and interfering with them. They got him though. Some woman swiped him with a baseball bat, knocked him out cold.' 'Then there was that woman raped in her own home.' 'And those that aren't evil are right wallies. A woman over the road has been nicking things out of her own house to get the insurance. Stupid slag, she should know that if you're going to do that, you should get somebody else to break in for you. That's common sense.' 'I don't want my Melanie to grow up to all this', says Lorraine, of the eldest daughter who remains with her. 'I want something better than that.'

But at least the chaos is outside Lorraine now, and not within, as it always has been in her life. She is happier than she has ever been. Paul owns a big transit van, for which he paid £48 six months ago. He has reconstructed it, and it is now worth £1200. Working on the van is his greatest pleasure. 'You get so involved, you don't have to think. Your mind is completely at peace.' He has welded a rectangle of strong metal on the bumper to strengthen it; there are six red brake lights at the back, the windows have been sprayed with silver reflecting paint. Inside, it is carpeted, with fleecy covers on the seats, a stereo and speakers. In the summer, they will take off in the van, tour the coast, be free. Sometimes Paul uses the van to tow vehicle breakdowns. 'You have to be careful, or somebody will see you and write to the Social to say you're working. That's the kind of mentality round here — they can't bear to see anybody get on.'

It was just before the 1987 election. Neither Paul nor Lorraine would vote. If they did, they would vote Conservative, but they don't see the point. They don't believe in politics; they believe in life, says Paul. And money. 'And love', adds Lorraine. On the day of the local elections in May, Lorraine met her mate. 'I asked her, "where you going." "To cast my vote". "Who you gonna vote for?" "I haven't a clue till I get there." "Silly cow."'

Within a couple of months, Paul left. When Lorraine was on her own, the house rapidly grew poorer and more shabby. The only income was £22 a week and Melanie's Child Allowance. Lorraine had given this to the 'veggy man' — the van that comes round the estate — to ensure that there is food and a packet of cigarettes for the weekend. She keeps Melanie at home with her, because she can't do without company. At the same time, she is concerned that Melanie is slow in learning to read and write. She is ten now. Lorraine has sent away for a leaflet about home-working. She has done this before, selling

135

jewellery, but all the pay was in jewellery, which she couldn't give away. Then she was selling handbags, but she had to buy all the merchandise first.

Melanie sits on the sofa in her night-dress. She eats two packets of fizzy fruit sweets, then with two bright pink lollipops paints her lips red. Lorraine has a man who comes to see her, but she has been too broken up by Paul's leaving her to want to start anything new. Her friend Kerry calls in. Kerry is depressed. Her five-year-old was hit by a stone that somebody threw at him; she took him to hospital, and during the tests they carried out, it was diagnosed that he has a bone disease. He is to be in plaster for at least the next eighteen months. On the day it was discovered that her little boy was sick, Kerry's boyfriend moved out of the house. 'He can't stand competition', she says, 'he wants all the attention for himself. He's like a kid. So he pisses off to somebody else who he thinks is gonna spoil him and look after him.'

Lorraine and Kerry have man-hating sessions to comfort each other. 'We're gonna start a meat factory', says Lorraine, 'cut men up and seal them in plastic and sell them to the butcher.' Kerry had been with one man for four years — unheard of durability in a relationship for her. He kept asking her to marry him, and she kept on refusing. At last, she accepted. 'Then the very night I said yes, he went out and stayed away all night. I got really worried. I thought something terrible must've happened to him. I rang up all his friends. Then at five in the morning, one of his mates arrived in a van. He said 'Hop in.' He didn't say anything, just drove me to this house. He opened the door, and there was my Tony in bed with another woman. I couldn't understand it. Why had he gone on and on asking me to marry him, and then the minute I said yes, just fucked off?' 'Some men are like that', says Lorraine, wise; 'they're fascinated just as long as they don't get everything they want.'

Kerry has seen Paul in the park. He had left Lorraine, first for the daughter of the man he was working for, and then for a woman of thirty-seven, whom he has now also left. He said, 'I've lost the two people I care most about in the whole world.' On the day he walked out of here, he said to me "Look after Lorraine, Kerry, she's special to me." I thought, if she's so special, what are you doing, leaving it to someone else to look after her?' Lorraine says 'I could never have him back. It was the lies he was telling me. He never even used his own name to me. His real name is Scott. He told me he was in the army, and he never was. His family slung him out. He used to come home and tell me the van broke down. When he went out of here, he took part of me and Melanie with him. It was like ripping something out of me. I'll never forgive him for that. He broke our hearts. I'll never be the same again. In the past, I've always gone straight off to find someone else. I thought I'd settled down with him. Trouble was he hadn't settled with me.

'I'm twenty-seven. I've had enough of the life I've led . . . Because I have tattoos, I wear jeans and a leather jacket, to men, that's like having a big sign up saying you're available. I want to get away from here, make a new start. I was at a friend's house one day, and two little girls were wheeling this baby in a buggy. I stopped and I was playing with him; later on, I found it was *my* baby, my little Stevie, and I didn't even know him. I don't think I'll ever have my other kids back now. They've settled where they are, and the people have got money, but I just keep wondering if they're getting the love they need. When you have a baby, if you've never been loved, you think "I want someone for myself, to give them all the love I've got."

'Kerry and me are like sisters. We can tell each other everything. The only man I have any time for is my brother. He works in London, on the buildings. He's the only man I know who isn't a bastard. He comes to see me and Kerry. He won't have anything to do with sex now, because of *Aids*. My father hasn't got long now; I shall be glad when he's gone, after what he done to me.

'Melanie is very understanding. Sometimes, when I'm

crying, she'll come and put her arms round me and say "Don't cry Mum." There's not many kids of that age show so much understanding. I want her to learn from my mistakes. I don't want her to go through all I've been through. I always seem to get men who finish up hurting me, from my father on. I don't want it. Maybe I ask for it, but I don't want it.'

Sky Channel plays on the black-and-white TV set: pop music and videos, Top Twenty songs repeated over and over. Lorraine gets Melanie to make tea; there's no sugar. 'We can't afford it. I really thought Paul was going to hold on to me, keep me under control. I know that's what I need. He kept accusing me of going with somebody else, when it was him that was doing it all the time.'

Three months later, Lorraine had moved; back into the estate where she had grown up. The week she moved in, she, her sister and Melanie spent an evening decorating. They were all slightly drunk, with the result that all the wallpaper was crooked and jagged. Lorraine had stood on a coffee table that collapsed beneath her, and its remains lie sprawled on the floor. The house is a 1930s semi that has been converted into two flats, in an area of the city known as a dumping-ground for problem families. You can never get credit with an address down here. Lorraine couldn't stand it on the new estate: too many memories. Her friend Kerry had got married, but her husband left her almost immediately. Kerry is pregnant, and Lorraine knows it is her own brother's baby. He was killed on Christmas Eve, driving home from work at 6 a.m. He was over-tired, and the bike hit a lamp-post. 'I never knew over Christmas, they never told me. But it was funny, all the holiday I was feeling irritable, kept getting mad at Melanie for no reason. I even slapped her round the face. Then I said "sorry babe" and burst into tears. Something was telling me . . . I want to get in touch with him. I might go to a spiritualist meeting. Tell him I'm sorry. He used to go with Kerry, she wanted to marry him. He said, "Wait two years." Then she went and married Simon, and it didn't last five minutes. He was the only man who's ever cared for me and didn't want anything from me.'

'I exchanged this house with a couple who lived here. When I left the other place, I felt as if I'd been let out of prison. The guy who lived here, he keeps coming round and saying he fancies me. I'm sure I was in prison with Carla, his wife. She kept asking me what it was like inside. I thought, "You should know." She hasn't told him: she's pregnant. The last thing I want to do is split them up. One of my mates went off with the man who drove the furniture van the day her and her husband moved. I'm finished with all that.'

Lorraine has seen Paul twice. 'As a matter of fact, I slept with him a couple of times. He wants to come back, but I won't. He thought that all it needed was to sleep with me a couple of nights and I'd be a pushover. I don't want to get hurt. I got my own back. I said to him, "I really like you Dave". He said "My name's Paul". I said "No it isn't, your real name's Scott." He gave me crabs. I got rid of them with a bottle of Dettol. I smelt like a drain. I also got all these blisters inside me. I think it might be herpes. Thank God I've got Melanie. She and me, we're like friends. She won't screw around like some girls. If she does, she'll get murdered.'

Melanie says 'I won't anyway.' Melanie is ten. Lorraine says 'I can tell her anything.' Melanie is eating two packets of Polo mints.

Lorraine's former boyfriend Butch is coming out next month. He's done two and a half years. He murdered a tramp in the park: he got a light sentence because he was on drugs at the time. 'As long as he doesn't find out where I am. He could do it again. He's a psychopath. He was injecting himself, so they got him with manslaughter. He's a menace. He'll do it again. He's had four psychiatrists since he's been in there. None of them can get through to him. Nutter. Don't I find them. Or do they find me?'

Lorraine has also been writing to Jack, also in prison. He has been in for attempted murder. 'But nothing like

Butch. His mate Troy had grassed him up. He set out to knife him, but got the wrong guy in the dark. He was sorry. He's a nice guy. Trouble is, I've been writing because I'm soft-hearted, and his letters have been getting more and more sexed-up. He thinks I'm waiting for him. Oh well, I'll worry about that when it happens. Got enough for one day.'

Welfare estate

The horror stories that make headlines in *The Sun* are matters of daily conversation on the poor estates: parents who let their kids sniff glue at home because at least they know where there are; the video-club man who sells his list of customers to house-breakers; the child of thirteen pregnant with a child allegedly from her own father. If you listened only to these, you could imagine that the poor have been brought to the edge of barbarism. The point of such tales is that they fill the empty hours of long-term poverty and unemployment. It is easy to ignore what is taken for granted, and that is the fortitude, the resource-fulness, and the sheer survival of the majority of the people.

Twice a day Mr Taylor takes the bus into the centre of town to do some shopping. He comes back with two bags full of tinned food, tea, sugar, sweets, ice-cream, soap, washing-up liquid, biscuits, meat and sausages. He is working for the Beddowes Road Youth and Community Group — twenty-five families who pool their resources each week, do their shopping in bulk, and save themselves between £2 and £3 a week in the process.

Mr Taylor was a sergeant in the army; later, he worked on the railways, and finished his working life after three heart attacks in a drop-forge. To keep himself active and feeling useful, he has organized the shopping for all those on benefit — that is for most of the people in his part of Beddowes Road, reputedly one of the poorest streets in the town. Each family pays 25p per member, and there is a draw each week with a prize of £5. At Christmas there will be £10 for each child and a hamper for every mother. In summer, there is a trip to Blackpool or Alton Towers. The savings are considerable: at the local supermarket, a tin of beans costs 4p more, a tin of tomatoes 8p, coffee costs a third more than in the big stores in town. The only thing Mr Taylor won't deal in is cigarettes. The kitchen is full of surplus stock: crisps, snacks, tins of peas, bags of sugar, packets of tea.

His achievement is the more remarkable because the family has had a long reputation of being 'trouble.' Mrs Taylor, a vigorous woman of fifty-seven, says 'When people are poor, they have to take it out on somebody. One of my lads used to be a fighter and got into some bother.' Ever since then, her boys have been consistently blamed for everything. There have been fourteen children, so it's been going on for a long time. There was once even a petition to get the family moved. 'It's my Mark at the moment. He's been accused of everything under the sun, from assault to arson to putting people's windows in. One woman accused him of sexually assaulting her; the police came to pick him up — he'd been in Blackpool for a week. When he was supposed to have set fire to some house, he was in hospital. It'll be Neil's turn next. This is one reason why we wanted to do something. People have got to stick together. The kids get blamed for everything. When everybody starts blaming kids, it means only one thing — the adults have given up responsibility.'

The estate is bordered by a marshy green and the mournful stretch of the cemetery railings. In November, the grass is dead and the colour is fading from the gardens. The sale of about one house in ten leads to some cruel contrasts: leaded lights, a Georgian door and a chandelier next to boarded windows and ragged curtains and overgrown gardens. At the back of the houses there are pigeon pens, a goat or even the occasional horse, Jack Russell terriers and German shepherd-dogs, the carts of tatters. The adverts for cockatiels and canaries for sale, the rabbits hanging in brindled bunches outside the shop — everything suggests the way of life of people who have never become completely urban; a long tradition of making do, where for many people not to make a bit on the side would be incomprehensible, even if it's only breeding a few birds, collecting scrap or second-hand clothes. The inventiveness and creativity of the people mocks the bureaucratic leaglism of government departments.

Winnie is a survivor. She lives in a cul-de-sac from which gates and fences have long been removed for pigeon-lofts or firewood. The number of the house is painted in bold white on the redbrick wall. Winnie is sixty-five. She has had sixteen children and two miscarriages. There are thirty-two grandchildren, and she always manages to buy each one a birthday card, notwithstanding the fact that she and her youngest son, David, are living on an income of £39.80 a week. David has had his benefit withdrawn. When he was called for interview under Restart, somebody had written to DHSS, saying that he had been seen going off to work on two mornings in a red car. He was in fact helping out a friend who was office cleaning, and was paid a few pounds. His benefit will not be resumed until he informs the DHSS how long he worked for the firm and how much he earned. David did not even know the name of the company where his friend was cleaning, so there is nothing he can do about it. As a statistic on the unemployment register, he has ceased to exist.

Winnie lifts up her thick cardigan to show the wasting flesh of her stomach. 'We're starving cock', she says. Without conscious irony, she taps her packet of cigarettes. 'These are the only thing that are keeping me alive.' The house is in a bad state of repair: the lavatory is disconnected, the plaster has come away from the wall, exposing the brick beneath; the back door doesn't fit.

Winnie has always led a chaotic life, though now she is, for the first time, deeply depressed. She is a small woman with thin grey hair. She has no teeth and a cleft palate, so it is not easy to understand what she says.

The children in the street torment her, put 'filthy things' through her letterbox. Today, Monday, Winnie's daughter Mary is here: she lends her ten pounds until she draws her money mid-week. This means that at least today there will be one proper meal. On Sunday all that Winnie and David ate was a boiled egg each. In a plastic bowl by Winnie's chair are the onion peel and carrot scrapings. The vegetables are cooking in water on the stove. To add to them there is a tin of mincemeat, which stands on the arm of the chair together with the other items of grocery that Mary has brought: a pound of lard, a bag of potatoes and a tin of peas.

Winnie has always collected little ornaments: the shelves around the walls are full of little glass animals, brass and porcelain. The visitor from Social Security told her she should sell them before asking for any more public money. This made Winnie very angry: the ornaments are clearly symbols; her longing, perhaps, for a life that is more ordered and delicate than anything she has ever known.

The house was recently broken into, money taken from the electricity meter. The fuel companies in this area have concluded that 83 per cent of meters are done by the people who live here (on what evidence it is difficult to say.) Unless there is a conviction in the courts, the consumer is considered to have been responsible and his or her account is debited with the loss. If there is a conviction, it is up to the customer to write to the gas or electricity board, requesting the account be cleared. Even when there is a conviction, the victim is frequently not informed; and when someone is done on specimen charges, all those that are taken into consideration rarely lead to the customer's debt being cleared. In any case, the gas was cut off in Winnie's house ten years ago; the rent arrears are irrecoverable.

David's only relaxation is playing darts. He practises on the much-used board on the kitchen door. On the shelf there is a trophy he won last year, a silver-gilt medallion mounted on a wooden stand — a tangible achievement in a world that has denied him so much. He doesn't go to the pub so much now, because he can only afford a half a pint, and can never return drinks. But he still practises every day. His great hero is John Lowe.

Mary's children have just come out of school; in the house, there is an eager opening of bags — Jelly Tots and crisps and bars of Flake. It is a celebration of the family being reunited at the end of the day, mother's gift to the children's return, the sad emblems of such love being tit-bits of value-added junk-food. Mary's own teeth are grey and decaying — a shocking sight in her smiling twenty-seven year-old mouth.

An extension has just been added to Mr and Mrs Howard's house for their fifteen-year-old son who is severely handicapped. Kenneth had encephalitis when he was eight, the result of a virus when he had measles. He is lying on a bed, suffering at the moment from a dislocated hip, which means that the leg has to be tied to the foot of the bed with a crepe bandage so that he does not move; he also has a chest infection. His mother sits in the chair beside him feeding him milk pudding. His legs are so thin that you can see the shape of the joints through the flesh; his fingers and toes are almost translucent. His eyes are half-closed, so that all you can see are the half-moons of the whites beneath the lids. Mrs Howard says 'We're not giving up. He can be his own worst enemy. Some days he will lose interest in everything, won't bother to eat, then the next day he'll perk up. He has a teacher comes in for an hour a day, moves the mobiles, tickles him. Although he can't speak, she has found out he can hear and smell. Part of his brain is waking up. I'm going to get him on his feet again. We went to see the specialist about his hip. He suggested amputation. I'm not having that.' Kenneth's parents sleep on the sofa in the same room.

Mr and Mrs Howard have seven other children. Mr Howard became redundant just as Kenneth contracted encephalitis. He lost his job in the shake-out from the

West Midlands engineering companies: there used to be 15 thousand people working in Darlaston, now there are less than 3000. He hasn't worked since. It would be difficult for him to do so — looking after Kenneth is a full-time job. At the moment Mr and Mrs Howard are getting no sleep. Kenneth is awake all night, screaming with the pain of his hip. 'The teacher tells us to try to concentrate his attention; sometimes you can, others, you feel him slipping away from you.' Mr Howard is waiting for the building to settle before he decorates and puts up posters of Liverpool football team. Football is Kenneth's passion.

On the poor estates, there is a higher concentration of all social wrongs: more crime, more handicap, more psychiatric illness, more drugs, more unemployment, more sickness. Ken Thompson, neighbourhood officer, is angry that the government claims to be treating more people than ever before on the National Health Service, and even issues figures to prove it. 'All this means is that they're shifted from hospital before they should be after the operation. They're being sent home, often to places that are inadequate and unsuitable.' He shows a photograph of a woman of eighty-seven, who was sent out of hospital four days after an operation for breast cancer; a large ugly wound. There was nowhere she could be looked after. 'I spent the whole day ringing round looking for a bed for her. After cajoling and threatening and pleading, she was taken back to the hospital that had discharged her. She died not long afterwards. The resources have not been given to the poor communities to help them cope. They go home too soon, they die of delayed shock or neglect or loneliness. Just because nobody can dispute their figures, the government gets away with it. But these are the consequences — you hear nothing about who has to pick up the pieces. There you are —' Ken Thompson says bitterly, throwing the photograph of the old woman onto the table, 'that says it all. Mrs Thatcher's cuts.'

Mr and Mrs Gillespie have been reduced to living in one room of their house; but to move would be, as she says 'the death of us.' She is in her sixties, he has Parkinson's disease, and can move only with the help of a Zimmer. Their daughter has just been admitted to psychiatric hospital; their son visits once a week. There is a big double bed in the room with an orange nylon counterpane. There is coal in a cardboard box labelled Ferguson TV, and the fire is blazing up behind its close-mesh guard. There are four cats and a dog in the room, sitting on the sofa in front of the fire. The curtains have not been opened. 'He can't be left', says Mrs Gillespie, 'but then, where would I go? I can hardly walk with sciatica.' On the walls are the faded, tinted photographs of their wedding. 'Didn't we make a handsome couple. I can't believe it when I look at us now, how your life gets smaller and smaller until it can be held in four walls.'

Sharon is on her own with four children, a girl of eight, a boy of seven, and the twins who are three. A thin young woman, still only in her early twenties, she sits on the sofa with her knees up to her chin as though cold, even though the gas fire is at full heat. Sharon's own dissatisfaction with herself is seen in the images around the room: a plastic effigy of a Botticelli-type Venus, two paintings of women with full breasts in negligées, and a big picture of a women up to her thighs in water, with a 1970s hairstyle and a red drape below her navel. The twins have a care order on them. Sharon resents the policing role of the Social Services, but at the same time she feels insecure as a mother. She is afraid of her inability to get the children to do as they're told. They won't go to sleep at night, and so she has fixed catches to the bedroom doors so they can't get up once they've been put to bed; but she knows this is a sign of defeat for her. She is afraid of Christmas, because she won't be able to give them what they want; she is afraid of the future because as they grow bigger, she may not be able to control them. The other day, the seven-year-old had the little Jack Russell terrier zipped up in his sleeping-bag. 'It was yowking, sounded like it was choking to death. He was enjoying it. He won't listen to me. There is a streak of evil in that boy.'

What doesn't show is the heroic efforts that have gone into surviving, into keeping together families that might so easily have been split up. The energies and resources of women that have been used are not easily discerned in the often scruffy and makeshift interiors. The battle against chaos is almost, yet never quite, lost each day. Yet at the end of the evening, Sharon sits back; the children are quiet. She makes coffee and watches TV for an hour, before settling down on the sofa with the dog for warmth and company. By eleven o clock the estate is silent and almost deserted. The habits of a working lifetime are not broken, even here, where unemployment is over a third in places.

In most houses the TV is on. People watch only distractedly while doing other things — household chores, talking, knitting, sleeping. The programmes are interrupted by the succession of Christmas adverts — computers for children, toys and gifts; microwave ovens, jewellery, cars and household goods, promoted by Santas and snowflakes and glitter. In the context of this poverty, these things look like a taunting of the people, a reproach to them, a reminder of their marginal status. But they don't see it like that at all. They are too busy surviving even to notice it. It isn't even cruel, for it is simply irrelevant to their lives.

Picking up the pieces

The people of Moulsecoomb felt they had enough publicity in the summer of 1986 to last a lifetime. The murder of two little girls in parkland opposite the estate on the edge of Brighton brought reporters here in force; and what they took away was both false and insulting to those whose lives are anchored here, and who couldn't just leave and forget, even if they had wanted to. It's the same with any place where there has been great grief or violence. 'They come and show the world what a terrible place it is, then the world can think "Oh well, what can you expect." It was the same with Handsworth or Broadwater Farm.'

There is a tree in the Wild Park that became a shrine to the children; the flowers are still renewed from time to time. People say 'It was a nightmare', 'It was like something you see on television.' In the aftermath, fear and anxiety were intense. 'You looked at every stranger and wondered. You even looked at your neighbours — there's something funny about most of us if you look hard enough.' Above all, people didn't let their children out of their sight.

Moulsecoomb, built between the wars, lies in the folds of the Downs behind Brighton. Streets are tiered into the hillside, well-spaced, a steep curtain of grass behind, the brush and undergrowth on the undergrowth of the Park on the other side of the Lewes Road. It is true that there are many people here oppressed by poverty and unemployment. There is a higher than average number of children in care; family breakdown is not unusual. You can't get hire purchase with an address here; you are more likely to get a job if you omit Moulsecoomb from the application form. But for all that, the vast majority of people are good parents and neighbours, struggling to make a decent life. And they know quite well what is wrong with the estate — they've been trying to tell the authorities for years. As Dave Barnard of the Tenants' Association says, 'It took something like this for Moulsecoomb to be "discovered". The forgotten city, lost in the Downs.' And it turns out, in the wake of the tragedy, that the local authority was just on the point of doing what the tenants have been campaigning for for twenty years.

'I came here with my wife and three children in the '60s. We had been living in a one-bedroom flat. It felt like heaven. A rather flawed heaven; a lot of the houses hadn't been touched since the thirties — stone sinks, draughty, cold.' Visitors to Brighton rarely go to Moulsecoomb. One woman said 'I don't go to Brighton much either. You try getting on a bus with three small kids, pushchairs and bags of shopping, fifty pence each way.' The town centre is three miles away.

Dave Barnard says he has been blacklisted by employers because 'I've never been able to keep quiet when I see an injustice. And because I've seen a lot of them I've made a noise.' Not that he has no work — the Tenants' Association is a full-time job, even though unpaid. 'When we were kids, we knew what our destiny was — work and yet more work. My father worked till he was seventy-nine, in spite of having his legs run over one day when he was working in the road. Now, nobody knows what to expect for their kids.'

'My last job was at the Polytechnic. I was caretaker and shop steward. We formed an inter-union committee, not just manual workers, but lecturers, technicians. That was dangerous. Jobs were being cut, and the union instructed us not to take on extra work. I was given work which they knew I'd refuse to do. I was dismissed for misconduct.

'The rubbish that was written about Moulsecoomb — we're all feckless and idlers, waiting for the next handout. Look at the paper:' — *The Sun* has a headline about people who had tried to get money from the Zeebrugge Ferry disaster by claiming their relatives had died — 'that's not news. Where's the news about those who helped and comforted each other, they far outnumber one or two wrong'uns. What's the message of the press — Expect the worst of strangers and less than the best from those you love. In whose interests is it to divide people like that?'

A number of people on the estate said they feel they are prisoners in their own home — the old people who don't go out in the evening, the children compelled to stay indoors since the murders, and especially the women with small children. To overcome this, there are three branches of COPE in Moulsecoomb. The meeting I went to, in a dilapidated prefab, was a chaotic and cheerful coming together of about eighteen women and twenty-five children. All the women agreed that if they had a choice they

149

would prefer to be working; yet none of them is registered unemployed. If the experience of women here is repeated all over Britain, there is, as many suspect, vast invisible force of unemployed women who don't figure in the statistics. Even if there were jobs, they say, travelling to and from the estate would take up half the pay, and you'd never be back by three o'clock to fetch the children from school.

Lorraine regards her experience as not unusual. Her husband left her with three children. It wasn't his leaving that she complains about, but the isolation. 'I was on nerve tablets, like a lot of women. I'd do the housework in half an hour, then I knew there was nothing till after school. Sleep was my escape. I'd go to bed and set the alarm for three o'clock. The fact that I can talk about it now shows how far I've come.' She has her son with her today, a pale ten-year-old, off school with a kidney infection. He wants to go into the RAF when he leaves school. Her other boy wants to be a doctor. 'My daughter — you know what her ambition is? She wants to be like her auntie, have a baby and stay at home on the social. She is eight.' Another woman says that boredom is the worst enemy. 'Make yourself tea and toast, listen to the phone-ins, read the paper, pick up some knitting. My life was like that for years. Until I started coming here, I thought there was something wrong with me because I hated it.'

Lorraine won't go into debt. She gets £70 a week. She won't use moneylenders, because she had enough of that when she was a kid, hiding behind the door when the debt collector came, telling him 'Mum's out', when she was sitting under the table.

Jean has loan from a company which she took to get clothes at Christmas, paying back £5 a week. 'When I can. He knows he can't get blood out of a stone, so he doesn't try.' Jean, a big placid woman with corn-coloured hair and an attractive Sussex accent, has seven children. Her husband has been out of work for five years. 'It's easy for the men. They can walk out. He plays cards with his mates. If I want to go out, he will stay in, but I have to ask first. He never asks. He just says "I'm going out now". We have a hen night once a month, you know, men, sex and babies. I get in, maybe twelve o'clock. He's been sitting there since seven, he says "Make us a cup of tea and a sandwich, love." It's not that he can't do it, it's just not his job. We get £50 a week on the social, plus £4 child allowance. Nine of us.'

To get free of loan sharks, some women have joined the newly formed Moulsecoomb Credit Union. Set up by an independent community group, PACT (People and Churches Together), it is the first parish-based credit union in Britain. It isn't easy, because so many people have to live from day to day, from Giro to child allowance, with nothing to spare for savings. Before the credit union can make a loan, the member must save £50; but the interest is only one per cent a month, compared with twenty per cent some are paying to loan companies. The stories of debt are familiar — people's benefit or pension books illegally confiscated as security, families selling the goods they took the loan for, getting deeper into a spiral of debt to pay for things they no longer own.

Anyone who lives in Moulsecoomb parish can join. The parish was chosen because there must be a bond of association between the members. Many credit unions are work-based — the police, London taxi-drivers — some are church groups. The Union pays dividends to savers after two or three years. Jackie Steer, organizing from a cramped office in St Andrew's church hall on the estate, says 'A credit union isn't an alternative: it couldn't exist if the NatWest were not there paying interest on a deposit account. But it's a modest redeployment of existing resources.

'We've fifty members so far, and aim to reach 500 after a year. There are fifty-two different social organizations in Moulsecoomb: if we had ten people from each we'd reach the target. At the end of a year we'd have £32 500, if they all saved £1 a week. It's hard to sustain because of the pressure people live under. But it's also a process of education, liberating ourselves from finance companies, and building up social relationships at the same time.'

In spite of adversity, people are not simply victims. They fight back. Nobody could have had a harder life than Val Marriott, but this hasn't impaired her warmth and generosity. Now in her mid-thirties, she works as a COPE playleader. 'We've some lovely people here. I wouldn't live anywhere else.

'I was brought up in a children's home. I've only recently come to terms with my childhood. For years I kept it all inside. I was abandoned on a railway station when I was ten. My mother died, and I was brought from Ireland to live with her husband, who by that time was living with another woman and her three children. He said I was too much like my mother, and he couldn't bear to have me in the house. I was taken by one of my brothers and left on the station. The years I spent in the home were numb. Starved of love. When I left I was looking for affection. If anybody pays any attention, you think it's love; men abuse you, they leave you, and that's how you learn it isn't love.

'For years I was addicted to anti-depressant tablets. And I used to drink. Then recently I found my family again for the first time in twenty-one years. It was a mistake. You keep this fantasy of a family to feed your emotions, then you find out it's false. In the home I was told my father had died, but I knew in my bones they were lying. I went over to Dublin to meet him. He didn't recognize me, he remembered me as a little girl with pigtails. Too much time in between.

'I had a breakdown when my eldest was about four. I can't remember anything, except that I lay on the sofa for about three weeks. Then one day I opened my eyes, and he was looking at me. He said "Mummy, what's wrong?" I dragged myself up, I couldn't bear the way he looked at me. I had so much anger inside me. Whenever I got angry with the children, I felt I hated them. I was frightened of my anger. I even had him put on the at-risk register. I didn't realize the anger came from my own childhood; it was rage against my own parents, for dying, for abandoning me. I know the difference now. One day I just threw the tablets away. My boy said "Mum you're so much nicer now."

'My husband has been wonderful. I can tell other people how much I love him, but I can't say it to him. If I said it, I'd be afraid he'd go away like the others. When you do find love, you daren't say anything for fear of losing it.'

Val has been strengthened through suffering. She now has three children, the youngest almost four. Her husband works as an electrician, and they are buying their house. She says 'I'm committed to this place. All my friends are here. To me, Moulsecoomb is the place where I learned to be happy.'

Marcus Ronchetti is vicar of Moulsecoomb and Coldean. After the murders there was, he says, bitterness and anger, a desire for vengeance; but there was courage and love too, and people have become closer. He detects a quickening of interest in the life of the spirit, 'a thirst for something more satisfying than the crude materialism that we are offered. In the parish magazine I placed a notice, inviting people to get in touch if they would like to talk about God. I had forty replies in two weeks. I don't like the idea of the vicar talking about everything under the sun except religion. Many children in Moulsecoomb had never been inside a church, had little idea of the meaning of God. A lot of people feel that religion is alien to them; and yet the place is full of people caring for each other; if you suggested they had a vocation from God they'd probably deny it.

'At the time of the murders, many blamed God for letting such a thing happen; but with time, there has been forgiveness. The families accept that their children have gone to God; desire for revenge has faded. I can honestly say this is the friendliest place I've ever lived in. I'm happier than I've ever been, and I don't say that lightly — I had a happy childhood, I was happy at college. You couldn't find a more decent community.'

Barry Lacock is a social worker in Moulsecoomb. Energetic and committed, he insists 'We don't see a collection of needs and problems that have to be answered. We see people doing things, running groups, being foster-parents, helping in one context, perhaps needing help in another. It's a two-way process; Social services shouldn't be targeted on the residium, the hopeless cases, it's the involvement of everyone in the community Moulsecoomb Neighbourhood Trust started out of a conversation with a woman on the estate who said she was bored and depressed. I said to her "What needs doing?" She said "There's no playscheme." "Is there anybody who could help you?" "Yes, my mate over the road."

'Great. We go to a local charity; we only wanted £50, they gave us £1000. We set some of it aside, and that's how the Neighbourhood Trust took off. We now handle £14 000 a year, employ a worker, organize holidays, celebrations. It's run through a management committee, all local people. Half represent local groups, the other half estate-based workers.

'Work has to be collaborative. There are three kinds of attitudes to estates like Moulsecoomb. The first is to want to do something to Moulsecoomb, punish the people — *The Argus* was full of letters like that at the time of the killings. Then there are those who want to do something *for* the estate, that's a paternalistic, charitable impulse; and then there are those who want to do something *with* the people who live here.

'There's nothing turns people off more than talk about the *poor*. In the Social Attitudes survey, only three per cent of the people of Britain see themselves as poor. They say defensively, 'I'm not poor', because they are fighting for their dignity. Politically inconvenient for the Left maybe, but that's how they feel.'

One day when I was in Moulsecoomb there had been an unexpectedly late fall of heavy snow. A family of five — parents unemployed, three young children — were holding hands and kicking the melting ice from a deep drift at each other. The woman said 'You be careful what you say about Moulsecoomb. Don't tell everybody it's too wonderful, or we shall have all the miserable buggers from Hove wanting to move in on us.'

Living on the margin

A house on a post-war council estate on the fringe of a Midland town; the estate cuts into a cornfield, and looks over a shallow valley, on the other side of which is a village engulfed by bungalows with carports and plantations of miniature conifers. Christine lives at the far limit of the built-up area, almost a mile from the shops, and a bus-ride into town that costs 90p return. Christine is twenty; she has lived here for the past three years, with her son Simon, who is almost five. Tanya is two.

It is a warm Saturday afternoon. The television is showing a war film; the colour is blurred so that everything appears green. Christine is nursing Tanya on her lap. Tanya is unhappy, crying intermittently, asking for a sweet, a biscuit, her dummy. She throws her arms around and wriggles as Christine rocks her to and fro in the protective chamber of her body. Christine is looking after her for two weeks, while her mother serves fourteen days in gaol for soliciting.

The house is well-kept and comfortable; oatmeal-coloured carpet and curtains, table and chairs of tubular steel and smoked Perspex. A large vase stands on the floor with coloured pampas grass and russet and green oats and barley. The window is open onto a strip of grass, from where the voices of children can be heard, playing and then quarrelling. Simon keeps returning to the open window. His mother lifts him into the room. Christine sits

155

back on the sofa; the springs have collapsed, so she is virtually sitting on the floor.

She is the fourth of a family of five. Her mother and father were unhappy together, and she became the object of many of their disputes, her father constantly beating and punishing her, her mother protecting him. When she was in her early teens, she ran away from home several times, and at thirteen was taken into care. Her father left the family, and her mother moved to Coventry to live with her boyfriend. Christine went to join this new household.

She became pregnant at fifteen and left school. The father of the child didn't want to know; and although she didn't realize it at the time, she cared for him quite deeply. In fact, she says sadly, he was the only person she has really loved so far in her life. She continued to live with the mother and the mother's boyfriend; but she and the baby had to share a room with her twelve-year-old sister, and the baby's crying kept her awake.

Christine moved back to her home town to live with an older sister who was married; but when her sister became pregnant, Christine had to move out. She applied for a council flat, but was not entitled to one because she was under 18. She lived in a series of hostels, in one of which Simon got gastroenteritis; he spent some time in hospital. Christine stayed with a friend for a few days before returning to emergency accomodation. While she was there, she met a girl who told her how easy it was to get money through prostitution. At first, Christine paid no attention. but it stayed there, in the back of her mind.

Two months later, she was rehoused in a flat. There was no furniture, no cooker. 'The Social gave me a grant for a cooker and a bed, but nothing else. There was no heating and it was the middle of winter. My Mum helped a bit. One night, I sat here and I hadn't a penny. No food, nothing for the meter. That was when I thought about what this girl had told me. I couldn't go and shoplift, because, well, I couldn't. I'd borrowed some money from friends and couldn't borrow any more. So I thought I'd go and see if it was that easy. There's a pub, The Angel, where a lot of girls go, but you get too well-known there. I couldn't do that. So I thought I'd try the street.'

In the centre of the town there is an extensive development of flats, six or eight storeys high, built on the site of the old terraced streets. At the base of the buildings there are garages, rubbish chutes and a kind of courtyard. Three sides of the flats have access to roads. This is where the girls work from. Discreet, not too well lighted — the street lamps are frequently smashed — with enough shelter to hide from residents and the police. But it is a bleak, cold place.

Christine got someone to sit with Simon, and then caught the bus that would take her to the flats. 'A prostitute on a bus, it didn't seem likely. I was frightened and trembling. I thought I'd never do it. I went for a drink, and while I was sitting there, I realized I didn't have any choice. I'd got to go through with it. When I came out I saw there were quite a few cars, moving slowly round. I didn't see any other girls. A car stopped and a man asked me if I was looking for business. I said yes. He said 'Five pounds,' and I said 'All right' So I got in, and he took me somewhere and parked, and I done him in the car. I was more frightened than anything else. He turned out to be very nice, and he gave me £10. It only took a few minutes. And that sort of gave me confidence. I thought, 'That's great.' So I did another one and went home with £15. I was surprised how easy it was. The next night I went out again and stayed longer, got more money. I was in a terrible way by that time, because I was already having the rent paid direct to the council from the Social, and I was getting just £13 a week in my hand.'

Christine started to go out several nights a week. It seemed too good to last, but at least she could buy her little boy the things he needed. 'It's not brilliant, by the time you've paid a baby-sitter and everything, but it's better than being on the Social.'

It wasn't long before she was picked up by the police

157

for the first time. She was cautioned; and for two weeks was so frightened that she didn't go out. But by this time, she had come to depend on the money she was making; and hesitantly, she returned. 'The police are always driving round those flats, all night sometimes. They might follow the car you get into, and then when you park, the copper opens the door and says "You're under arrest." Only to the girl of course, whatever they say about being out to catch kerb-crawlers. The second time I was picked up, they took me to the police station. I really was scared then. I denied I was soliciting. If they can see you're young and new at it, they lock you in the cell, so you have to confess what you were doing. I was worried about Simon. They said "We're keeping you here all night." So I said yes, I was doing it, and they let me go. They were all right about it, but said next time I would go to court.

'I carried on, and wasn't caught again for a long time. Some nights they watch you, you know they've seen you, you think they're going to take you in, but they don't. It's almost like playing a game with you. Then I was picked up again and taken to court. It was six weeks before the court hearing, and during that time, I was picked up almost every other night. Once you're known, that's it. There were seven other charges by the time it came to court. You get reckless. You think "Oh well, the worst has happened, what else is there to lose?" I got a fine of £100, to pay so much a week. Well you've got no way of paying off that money except by going back to prostitution. It's a vicious circle. Next time I got a two-year probation order. The probation officer is quite nice, but he wants me to promise I'm not going to do it any more. It's the only way I've got of living, of giving my little boy the things he wants. What else can I do? There's no jobs, I'm not trained for anything. I was on the phone for a time, but I was cut off for not paying the bill. Things were easier then — I didn't have to go on the street, I could work during the day.'

Christine doesn't like to think about the future. If she

looks too far ahead, she gets depressed. Each day takes all her energy and effort. She says she just hopes something will happen — which means that she will meet someone who will look after her. That, she says, is the ambition of most of the girls. But the trouble is, meeting men as she does, it isn't easy to establish much of a relationship. You can't get to know them; you don't want to. Christine says she would carry on 'even if it was legal' — after a time it's impossible to imagine doing anything else.

Christine's unhappy childhood makes her talk as though the most significant part of her life had already happened; at twenty, there is a stifling sense of closed possibilities, of reduced expectations, hope used up. Sometimes she sees Simon's father: she did love him, but doesn't now. She hates being alone. Most of the time she is with Tanya's mother or with her Mum, who now lives in a flat in the same town, having broken up with her boyfriend. She has a brother at university, and a sister whose husband has his own business. 'She won't have anything to do with me. They found out what I'd done and that was that.'

Christine works two or three nights a week, but never at weekends. 'There's no business at weekends. The men are all at home with their wives and children', she says without bitterness. She does resent the injustice of the girls being arrested while the men get away with it. The girls are only answering a need, 'a demand. So why should we get blamed? It's not as if we were tempting men away from the straight and narrow. Why do the police waste so much time on us? Every night you open the paper, there's crimes of violence, mugging and robbery and murder — things they can't solve, so they go and pick up a few girls for soliciting, try and make themselves look successful.'

As she talks, Christine is still nursing Tanya. The child is restless, rubs her eyes with her fists, not knowing what to do with herself. Christine has told her that her mother has had to go away for two weeks; but this means nothing to the child. She gets angry, and hits out with her fists.

On the sofa is one of Simon's storybooks. She says 'Read it.' It is a story about an Impossible World; a little boy whose mother keeps telling him all about the things he cannot do, all the things that are forbidden or impossible. So one night he travels with his toy train down the rainbow to the world where impossible things happen, where candy grows on trees and fabulous animals live in the clouds. From his adventure he brings home a snow-flake that will never melt; so whenever his mother tells him something is impossible, he knows better. Tanya says 'Again.' Then she loses interest and starts crying again. Christine comforts her and says Mummy will be here 'soon' — that most treacherous of all words to children.

The ordinariness of Christine's life is what strikes you; the absence of glamour, the hours of boredom in being a prostitute on a council estate. What is even worse is that she is a single parent, an intelligent woman trapped, a lonely person. Everybody knows about her, of course: her misdemeanours have been amply reported by the local paper, which is a kind of refinement of the pillory in the community. Late afternoon: children are playing on the green; some boys are dismantling a motorbike; a woman sits on her doorstep. Nobody speaks, but everybody is watching. The neighbours don't trouble Christine. One of the mercies of living on this estate is that other people have too many problems of their own. The decayed sense of community here works to Christine's advantage; no one is inclined to throw the first stone. She says 'They call it being on the game. It's no game. Getting money is the most real thing there is.'

CHAPTER FIVE

Green politics and the poor

The poor, far from being expendable as some social critics have argued, are the object of the greatest solicitude in rich Western societies. This is not to say that they are loved, but that their presence is recognized as indispensable; and never more than in the midst of such wealth as might be capable of making them disappear for ever. It would perhaps be a more accurate formulation to say that although the poor may — indeed do — perish, poverty itself must survive.

So central is this vast and noble design to the deepest purposes of our society that the Conservatives — the conservers of precious little else in our time — have spared no effort in their conservation of poverty. It requires no great imagination to see that there is no problem of the poor in Western societies: the problem is with the rich, the contradictions of whose ideology the poor have been appointed to resolve for them.

The most implacable enemy of wealth is not poverty, but sufficiency; and this explains the profound, if reluctant, attachment of the rich to the poor. Given the plenty we have seen, the goal of enough for all would be the easiest thing in the world to attain. That so much energy has been expended in circumventing it should perhaps make us wonder at the threat that such a modest and humane objective might pose to our society and the values it is believed to embody. For such an achievement, whatever comforts and satisfactions it might bring to the people, would certainly spell ruin for the economy.

This is where the poor have such a vital role. They are not merely the foil, whose suffering goads the rich into the endless accumulation of more, but they also offer the sole moral justification for the necessary dynamic of continuous growth and expansion. For 200 years the rich have told us that the creation of wealth can alone alleviate poverty; and throughout those 200 years, the whole period of industrial capitalism, through the mightiest concentrations of wealth the world has ever seen, the poor have obdurately remained. The rich have told us an antique and familiar tale: inadequate resources alone dictate that many must remain poor. One day we shall see an end to the sorrows of the outcast and dispossessed. But not yet. The contemporary version of this reality is heard in the insistence that Britain is a poor country (despite being the sixth richest in the world), and that we cannot afford to keep our poor in the extravagant style to which they have become accustomed, that they have sunk into a cosy indigence from which it has been Mrs Thatcher's mission to rouse them. And in the project of enrichment, it must be the poor who pay. It is clear that whatever freedoms the free world may enjoy, either now or in the future, freedom from poverty is not going to be one of them.

In other words, the poor are the ideological hostage to the illusion that we live in a world of absolute (as opposed to artfully contrived) scarcity. Their misery acts as both deterrent and stimulus: they are the generators (principally in others) of the energy required to avoid their fate; and at the same time, they are permanent exhibits in the capitalist moral freak-show, whose elaborately induced privations may be further exploited to demonstrate the need for further and faster economic growth.

Perhaps the most remarkable feature of the intractability of poverty is not that it persists at all, but rather the manner in which the fiction has been maintained that we are still unable to produce enough to answer all our needs. As long ago as the 1840s, Thomas Carlyle observed that 'England is full of wealth, of multifarious produce, supply for human want of every kind; yet England is dying of inanition.' It has been the way in which the 'unabated bounty of England' has continued to grow without eliminating poverty, which deserves closer scrutiny than it has received.

For what could no longer be concealed from Carlyle in 1842 is far more obvious to the rest of us a century and a half later — that the wealth of Britain makes the survival of poverty not a natural phenomenon, but a carefully wrought artefact, a cunningly contrived condition, which has nothing whatever to do with scarcity and everything to do with ideology.

For it is absurd to maintain that it is the West's incapacity to produce that ensures poverty should be such a brutal and degrading visitation. Once the basic cause of poverty is removed (absolute dearth of resources), this must be replaced by the development of an artificially created and subjective sense of insufficiency, for nothing could be more menacing to industrial society than that the people should declare themselves satisfied with what they have. Such a simple and apparently desirable possibility must be avoided at all costs. And it is to this exalted end that the period of restless and violent transformation that we have lived through in our time has been devoted. The people — not just the poor, but all of us — have been reshaped, our sensibility reformed, our psyche remoulded in the interests of preserving a redundant (but ideologically essential) sense of our own impoverishment. Those who asked for nothing more than modest and frugal satisfactions have been overtaken by a more powerful compulsion, have been swept away in the unstoppable need of capitalism for endless and intensifying growth; and our fundamental and answerable needs have been broken and restructured in the image of a system that has nothing to do with answering them. It is no accident that the key figures of our time have been those manipulators of the ambitions of the people, the hucksters of fantasy and vendors of illusion, those makers of images and conjurors who have managed to create strange new forms of poverty out of the super-abundance that we paradoxically flaunt as our proudest achievement.

In this process, we have seen a remoralizing of the rich, a resanctification of wealth. The poor are no longer estranged from the rich as their mortal enemies, as the usurpers of the people's necessities, but have been clasped to them in so tight an embrace that the space has been closed between enough and plenty, the gap occluded between sufficiency and more. It is this conquered territory that requires to be liberated by political alternatives, for this marks the greatest of all colonial triumphs of capitalist conquest — its incursion into the inner spaces, the subduing and trampling of the country of the heart, the ravaging and reconstruction of the inner landscapes.

This is how it happens that the rich can now project themselves, not as plunderers and expropriators of the poor, but as their friends and allies, attached to them in a single shared desire for the wealth that will enrich us all. They offer themselves as models for imitation and emulation. In this process of rehabilitation, there has been a more frank veneration of wealth for its own sake than when it was draped in the more decorous deference to breeding, caste or station. When the rich become objects of universal admiration, other, more troubling questions are easily elided — whether, for instance, the rich really have appropriated for themselves the best of all human possibilities, or whether their idolatry is not an aberration that oppresses them also; in short, whether or not the best things in life really can be subordinated to the imperatives of buying and selling — all those questions traditionally subject to more searching spiritual arbitrators than those noisy proponents of that easier, and dominant morality that declares that if it makes money it must be good.

Is it any wonder that those who have sought to define 'adequate' or 'sufficient' standards for the poor have found themselves repeatedly thwarted? What they, for all their painstaking concern, have for the most part failed to appreciate is that there is no frontier so obligingly static as a 'poverty line'. The system from which they would wring such reasonable concessions as 'a decent income', 'a dignified standard of living' doesn't work in that way. It is a voracious and mobile process that never rests; so that even as more and more wealth is created, it is attended by the growth of subjective feelings of inadequacy. All increase brings a sense of enhanced privation. The alleviation of poverty becomes an heroically doomed task, because everything is poverty that is not total and absolute wealth. Before the ubiquitous show of riches in the West, all human beings are diminished and inadequate. This is why the rich themselves are never satisfied, but focus their discontents on all the things that even their wealth cannot quite reach. Deprivation is certainly relative, but what it is relative to is an incalculable, indeed infinite, quantity of money. Sometimes this awareness surfaces in our everyday lives — for example, in the homely cliche about keeping up with the Joneses, which so many of us give as a reason for striving beyond sufficiency. Who do we imagine the poor Joneses are trying to keep up with, if not those same inplacable, inhuman rhythms of an unlimited power to produce and offer for sale everything the heart could desire, and a great deal more besides? It is an ineffable contest, the outcome of which is a foregone conclusion, in which we, like the Joneses, will necessarily be defeated.

Poverty will persist, surviving both the most punitive legislation and the most assiduous philanthropy; and it is this trap that ensures the people whose lives are the subject of this book will not be rescued by any access of riches. It is not that the poor are still with us that should excite our wonder, but the sentimental belief that they could ever disappear from a society whose ideology places them at the very centre of its purposes; an arrangement that our oscillation between punishment of and charitable endeavour towards the poor is unlikely ever seriously to disturb.

Nothing could be more damaging to the Green cause

than the perception that it is supported by privileged people who have enough for their own needs, and are now eager to limit the access of the poor to those benefits of industrial society which they themselves enjoy. This is why the most urgent task is to show how and why the poor would be the chief beneficiaries of Green policies.

It is clear that the texture and feeling of poverty are modified at each successive stage of the developing (or mutating) economy. Yet even the welfare state — which was expressly designed to abolish want and insecurity — has proved incapable of curing the ills it came into being to remedy. What is at issue here, of course, is the belief that poverty, unemployment and want are symptoms of the failure of industrial capitalism, signs that it isn't working: on the contrary, they are absolutely necessary to its workings, and are indicators that it is functioning with the greatest efficiency.

Those who claim that there is anything easy about poverty in its characteristic contemporary form would be swiftly disabused if they were to be exposed to the fear, violence and stress of the ghettoes and slum estates. What are no longer irremediable scourges of nature — periodic absences of sufficient material resources — have been recreated by political art: insecurity and want, artificially contrived in a world of abundance, act as no less powerful a motivator upon all those who can struggle out of these cold, hard places as earlier forms of poverty did upon those who by their exertions managed to claw their way out of the slums and tenements of the nineteenth century city.

Our discussions remain haunted by the rhetoric and imagery of scarcity. The maintenance of illusions of insufficiency is as much part of the rich West as the creation of wealth. Indeed, the two are indivisible. As a result of this, every faltering of the economy, every recession — such as that of the early eighties — can be exploited to halo the ideology of growth and expansion once more, place it firmly at the furthest limit of all aspiration and hope. Because it is an undeniable truth that an absence of the resources to procure subsistence is a grievous assault upon human freedom, we have too credulously assumed that the obverse must also be true: that all liberty grows in direct proportion to the amount of money at the disposal of the individual, and that therefore, private wealth in superabundance must represent the ultimate emancipation. It is to upholding this basic proposition that so much of the popular press and television is devoted: the public worship of megastars and pop idols and sports heroes has nothing to do with talent, itself often modest but rather with the celebration of the cosmic freedoms which their riches confer on them.

Existing patterns of economic growth can never rescue the poor from their exclusion and deprivation. What growth means in practice is that more and more human experiences are capitalized and marketed, appearing in the world in the form of commodities and services. These supplant earlier ways of answering need, which become decreasingly available outside the market system. This is a process that always serves the rich rather than relieving the poor. The rising disposable income of the rich means that a great deal of ingenuity must be expended in devising ways in which they may spend it. Not only must new needs be uncovered, fresh wants awakened, whims and desires slumbering in the deepest unconscious be roused in such a way that some monetary exchange appears to satisfy them but also all kinds of ingenious requirements must be manufactured and implanted. Even profound yearnings that cannot be answered in this life must be guided and channelled, re-worked until they appear to approximate to some market-shaped commodity. It is not so much that the goods are delivered to the people, as that the people are delivered to the goods: the deepest human longings are caught up in marketed transactions, where they have no place, and are therefore doomed to repeated bitter frustration and failure. Our human substance has been caught up in the machinery of buying and selling, just as the bodies of workers in the early industrial era were sometimes trapped in the unguarded machine and whirled round and round by belts and wheels and pulleys; a mangling of our humanity.

Economic development signifies the passage of growing areas of human activity under the dominion of the markets. The result of this for the rich is that they find at their disposal agreeable and unexacting ways of buying in the satisfactions and distractions that were not previously available in this form; and they gain thereby a pleasant sense of enlargement in their lives, however dependent they may subsequently become upon this dynamic, however *unfree*. The poor (and this is true of the poor all over the world) have a quite different perception of market penetration. They discover that things formerly freely available, products and services offered outside the money economy can no longer be obtained as before: they have been appropriated and enclosed, demarcated and placed in displays of merchandise in shop windows, have been packaged or professionalized, transformed into the product of another's labour; and remain out of reach of their inadequate income. One consequence is that even when they become a little less poor, at times of great prosperity, they can never keep pace with the constant seizure of their necessities and their mysterious passage into the realm of the to-be-purchased: because the model of capitalist growth determines that the rich must get richer before the poor may become less poor, the rate of market penetration always far outstrips the modest rise in income of the poor. While the rich scan the enhanced range of merchandise, wondering how to spend their augmented resources, the poor only see more and more desirable — indeed, necessary — purchases recede from their grasp, just as the water and grapes withdrew from the outstretched hand of the tormented Tantalus. For the poor do not inhabit a separate culture from the rich: they must live in the same world that has been contrived for the benefit of those with money. And their poverty is aggravated by economic growth, just as it is intensified by recession and non-growth.

Moreover, in a society in which monetary exchanges expand, human resources shrink. As a result, no one can ever have enough for their satisfaction, and that includes even the wealthiest. The rich feel, not so much contentment with what they have; more a subjective sense of gnawing insufficiency: when everything is for sale, all humanity is impoverished. The necessity for economic growth in the industrial system expresses itself, indeed becomes fused with and ultimately indistinguishable from, the needs of individuals. This internalized estrangement from our own selves renders us all the more suggestible to the promptings of the industrial vending-machine to which our deepest desires and wantings are harnessed.

Whatever the wealthy may say about their devotion to economic growth for the sake of the poor ('levelling everybody up'), such virtuous show is a piece of hypocrisy: such an objective would require limitless money for everyone, in order that they might acquire the infinity of things for sale. The attachment of the rich to the poor in a shared desire for economic growth is calculated to cast all those who seek selective or alternative growth in the role of implacable enemies of the poor. Their true friends are, it would seem, those who are united with them in a common, symbiotic endeavour.

By liberating from the markets some of those things that are inappropriately held fast there, the poor would be the first to benefit. Anything that lessened the gulf between their purchasing power and that of the richest, would represent not loss but a vast relief. The less that commodities and services are subject to the transforming alembic of the markets, the greater will be the release of people's creative energies, inventiveness and imagination — those things that have become slow and somnolent, put to sleep by a culture where their only outlet lies through the suggestions of those with something to sell. Many of our powers and abilities lie dormant,

169

passive as a princess in a fairy tale who can be awakened only by a lover's kiss: only the magic touch of money, it seems, can infuse us with vibrant life.

The poor beat vainly against the limits of their purchasing power, like those confined in prison hammering against unyielding brick walls. If the rich are such ardent proponents of existing patterns of economic growth, this is not simply because this enhances their freedoms, it is because by means of intensifying market control, the poor remain more securely subordinated to them. This relationship, determined by the West, between rich and poor is replicated with perfect symmetry, all over the world. And its inescapable influence penetrates everywhere; not even the most self-reliant traditional societies can resist. What an irony it is that at the very time when the unsustainability of this form of development is becoming apparent, those societies which offer still, however faintly, the sketch of an alternative should themselves be in the process of being ground to extinction.

CHAPTER SIX

Sustainability threatened

Instead of eagerly learning from the sustainable practices in those few places on earth where they have continued without interruption for millennia, such precious examples are still being crushed by the necessities of the market system. Those whose way of life has been characterised by the most careful equilibrium with the natural world, and who have so much to teach us, are being mercilessly driven into the very economy that has degraded the rest of the natural world, and is now rendering their own tradition unsustainable. It demonstrates just how total and all-embracing the dominant economic system is: it can permit no other way to survive, even though the very survival of humanity may depend upon the retrieval and revalorising of such practices.

It isn't a question of nostalgia for the past; there can be no 'going back'; there is no myth of return. It certainly isn't a question of worshipping nature — nature has always been too harsh and cruel for that. It is, however, a matter of respect for the natural world, an acknowledgement of our dependency upon it, for which dependency upon money has become an ugly and brutalizing substitute. What we must find is an enriching symbiosis between humanity and the earth that can allow all people to live with dignity and sufficiency; and the adivasis — or tribals — can offer us a precious and living example — not to imitate, but to inspire and to give us the courage to work for our own emancipation.

The adivasis of western India

Talasari, 150 miles North of Bombay, is close to the Gujerat border; a cluster of tribal villages built on outcrops of red rock, huts of coarse grass and bamboo, reinforced with mud and cow-dung and surrounded by hedges of euphorbia and thorn. Wild morning glory and showers of cerise bougainvillea spill over the thatch. In the compounds grow plantain, mangoes and tamarind, from the seeds of which a tangy juice is made to give savour to the staple, rice. Oval-shaped craters of paddy-fields cover the landscape like links in a long earthen chain.

The adivasis were originally the owners of the land and forests. They lived outside the cash economy until dispossessed of their land by Hindu and Parsee landlords at the instigation of the British. It wasn't long before they became bonded labourers. One man recalls that his father had been a debt-slave for the sake of a fifty-paise loan he had been unable to repay. The adivasis were pushed back to the poorest land. They were compelled to do vethi, or forced labour. Half their produce was given to the land-lords. They still remember how people were mistreated by the rich: the man strung upside down over a fire of chillis for stealing a mango; women forced back to work within hours of giving birth; a man yoked to a plough in harness with a bullock.

Even the stories the adivasis tell of themselves show them as stigmatized: a god came down and went to ask the people for food. It was a time of famine. The first family he visited had nothing to give. 'Can't you see we're starving?' The same response from the second family, the third. Then he came to a moneylender who had a hoard of food, which he gave freely to the god. And that is why the adivasis were cursed.

Here and there you can see traces of the former land-owners' estates: in the middle of an empty field are concrete posts and a metal gate swinging on rusty hinges, once the ceremonial entrance to a great farm. In the 1940s, the Communist Party of India (Marxist) [the CPI(M)] led the adivasis in a series of revolts and uprisings, which culminated in the abolition of bonded labour. After Independence, under the Land Ceiling Act, the landlords had to sell off large holdings of land. Many found ways round it: there is no restriction on the land that can be used for orchards, and as a result there are vast plantations of papaya or rubber, with palatial houses in chickoo groves; others simply transferred land to their relatives; some maintained their power by becoming moneylenders.

The efforts of the CPI(M) at that time were heroic. It duly benefited from the people's gratitude, and the area was a party stronghold. But in spite of ending the worst abuses, poverty and oppression remained. Most families have to find work in the dry season in neighbouring towns, or in the brickfields (the region is full of ugly red scars where farmers have sold their topsoil to the brick industry.) When the monsoon comes they must work in their own fields, and they support themselves during this time by taking a loan until their own rice is harvested. In the rains, the nallas become torrents that can't be crossed, so they need to buy two or three months' provisions — chillis, dal, flour; and when there is sickness or a wedding, the moneylender is the only recourse at very high rates of interest. The CPI(M) came to take the people's support for granted. Big landowners themselves became prominent members — the powerful are not squeamish about the guise they assume in order to maintain their influence. The party also shows the limitations of so many Communist parties in its lack of understanding of the culture of the people it was eager to emancipate. Godavari Parulekar wrote a book about the struggles of the adivasis, in which she describes them as 'illiterate helpless creatures living in separate little huddles in hills and vales and jungles.' They were 'culturally backward', and it had taken the CPI(M) to rouse them from the slumber of centuries.

During the slumber of the CPI(M) in the early eighties, a few Jesuits gave the impulse to a new political grouping,

173

the Kashtakari Sanghatna or United Workers, articulating the contemporary grievances of the people after the fashion of liberation theologians in Latin America. There has been a Mission and school at Talasari since the 1930s, when some of the tribals were christianized. The Communist Party, seeing its strength threatened, accused the Jesuits of trying to convert people. There were a number of attacks on Christian villages by angry party members. The Kashtakari Sanghatna, drawing no doubt on memories of the messianic fervour of the old CPI(M) had raised great hopes among the people, promising revolutionary change and the imminent overthrow of the oppressors of the people. There was a big morcha, violence against the moneylenders and shopkeepers. The leaders were arrested, and expelled by the Jesuits, so that the Mission could distance itself from their activities.

In this tense political context, the Maharashtra Prabodhan Seva Mandal (MPSM) works with the tribal people: a rural and educational development project, led by a former atomic physicist, that seeks to revalorise the traditional culture of the adivasis, their respect for the environment, their sustainable economy, their vast knowledge of living and growing things. It is an enterprise that strikes not only against the values of conventional development economics, but also against the narrow economism of the Communists, as well as against the official State structures that are dedicated to the incorporation of the 'backward classes' into the mainstream of Indian life. Indeed, MPSM seeks to avoid all forms of colonizing people; not least because the culture of the adivasis offers an alternative to the attempts at development that litter and lay waste much of the countryside of Northern Maharashtra: ill-conceived dams which displaced more people than they helped, dairy schemes that depend upon imported breeds of cattle that are difficult and expensive to maintain, deforestation that has intensified the rain-shadow effect as well as removing a source of food and medicine.

Vasudha is collecting 'unknown' information about adivasis culture for MPSM. She lives in a hut in one of the secluded hamlets; a cool mud house pervaded by the sweet smell of grass and cattle; cattle, being the people's most precious possession, live inside the huts. Vasudha, herself a Hindu, nevertheless finds the Jesuits (at least in their contemporary form) the least 'colonial' of all the groups vying for the soul of the tribals. Of the adivasis, she says 'Their culture is as dense and involuted as the foliage of the forest; as impenetrable too. We are always learning.' Vasudha was a teacher in Bombay until she went to work as interpreter for a friend who was researching into adivasi art. 'The motifs of their paintings reflect the richness of the culture.' We visit a hut where a marriage has just taken place: on the wall, a chowk has been drawn, with a representation of Palghat, goddess of vegetation, a fertility symbol. There is a painter from this area, Jirya Soma Mase, who has become famous; his work is sold all over Europe.' Vasudha speaks with enthusiasm of the culture, when she tells of the 'kanseri puja, the song after harvest which is associated with the corn goddess. It is sung for three days, partly in the house and partly in the fields. It has no unity of time, space or location, but is part of an ancient epic, the narrative of which is not linear. The adivasis call themselves vanvasi, inhabitants of the forest. Nobody quite knows their origins, whether they are autochthonous, even pre-Dravidian. They see themselves as a separate religious group; the process of Hinduization is also a form of colonialism, just as the Christian missionaries were colonial, or the attentions of the Communist Party. The trouble is that the educational system makes them ashamed of their own culture, inferiorizes them, suppresses knowledge that is vital for their survival, and indeed could be vital for ours, if we really care about a sustainable future.'

Even the adivasi children know the names of hundreds of plants and trees and their uses, many of which have always supplemented a meagre diet of cereals and pulses.

They know which shrubs are good for fuel, lighting, medicine. They can make a malai, or wicker fish-trap for when the nallas are in flood; they catch shrimps in holes in the river bank by means of a powder made from tree-bark which acts as a narcotic. They can catch wild hare, quails and partridge, and they eat boras, wild fruits richer in vitamin C than any other. They know the use of ak or rui to ease fever, because its leaves are 10deg. C, cooler than the surrounding atmosphere; its lilac-coloured buds are used as hair ornaments. The fruits of the bhindi tree are good for jaundice; neem assuages sickness; jamun can be made into an inky paste to heal wounds and skin disease.

Winin Pereira runs MPSM and a documentation centre from his house in Bombay. He says 'For the adivasi a tree is not simply a tree: it is also a place where the ancestors lived. It is food, shelter, a meeting-place and a familiar landmark. It is fuel and fodder and a source of building material. An adivasi "reads" trees as a good reader reads words: in their entirety, at a glance. The botanist, on the other hand, reads trees as a neoliterate reads words — letter by letter.'

In the village of Savroli, part of the Talasari cluster, the paddy fields are parched by the February sun. A girl of seventeen, working in nearby brick-fields, is collecting toddy from the palm-trees: a thick milky juice that ferments lightly in an earthen pot and is mildly alcoholic. From a thatched hut set in a small bamboo plantation comes the sound of a woman keening. Her child died four days ago, and the neighbours are saying that she neglected the baby by leaving her with a child too young to look after it. In the late afternoon the women return from the forest with a headload of firewood, a walk of seven or eight kilometres each way. They must lay in a store of wood for the time when the rivers will be impassable. The thatch on the house must also he renewed before the rains, and the bunds must be built up around the paddy-fields.

Most of the huts have wide eaves, with wooden pillars forming a veranda. Inside, they are cool and spacious.

Nothing could be further from the image of backwardness associated in the Western mind with the idea of 'mud huts.' Anil Agarwal has said that 'of the various types of traditional building materials available, mud is the most widely used and will remain so long into the foreseeable future.' Available locally, it is cheap, climatically suitable, requires a minimum of labour and is aesthetically pleasing. A man whose parents had been bonded labourers shows us his house with pride. One corner is fenced off as a byre. The interior is uncluttered: storage vessels and palmyra mats; a stiff cape of strong grass used for working in the rain. The sun slants through a narrow aperture in the wall, illuminating the furls of sweet wood-smoke from the stove of three bricks. Three big vats of plaited straw reinforced with dung contain rice: one for use this summer, one for sowing, the third in case the harvest fails. Pulses are tied in bags hanging from the roof, secure against rodents. A baby lies in a cotton sling oscillating in the shade of the veranda; a granddaughter is threshing toor, a kind of vetch which gives off a fragrant dust; the pods will be fed to the cattle.

The adivasis formerly lived by barter to supplement those things in which they were not self-reliant, and they still exchange rice for dried fish, bombils and sardines, with the vendors who come from Bombay. But the market economy thrusts more and more deeply into their lives; the little shops in Talasari sell Britannia biscuits, Vim, Lifebuoy and Lux soap, sweets, bidis, cigarettes, Vick and aspirin. Many people now sell the wild grass that grows in the monsoon which goes to feed the milk-producing buffaloes of Bombay. This means that their own cattle must graze as best they can. In one field there is a dead cow. The vultures, always overhead, fly in regular circles; one sees the dead beast and descends; the others, noticing the gap in the sky, follow and swoop on the carcase.

Night in the village: a vast expanse of stars, the spectral white trunks of kakandul trees. The crickets rasp, a silver moon sends long shadows into the rocky hollows. The

177

children at night school are reciting Hindi after a day in the fields tending cattle or looking after younger children. Shanti, a widow of twenty-two with four children, who is working in Talasari for 150 Rupees a month, is slightly tipsy. A boy of eighteen tells how his family lost three cows last year; a seventeen-year-old talks of his ambition to join the army. A young man who has been a Kashtakari Sanghatna activist stumbles on the unlighted path. He stops when he sees us. Angrily he says 'Why have you come here? Why can't you leave us alone. What is the use of your development?' The village had been raided by the Communists, and many people fled in terror into the jungle. The defeat of the Kashtakari Sanghatna has dashed all the high expectations and left a legacy of great bitterness; the moneylenders, the employers of labour in the big orchards, the police and the officials are still in control.

In the school, the youngest children are making a model of their village. The teacher is keen to insert into the curriculum — a tight schedule pinned to the wall, with a month-by-month breakdown of the work officially required of her — a programme that will validate and reflect positively the children's experience. Among the older children, the demands of exams leave little space. Of a class of forty sixteen-year-olds, more than half expected to remain farmers; about a third wanted to be engineers or doctors. Only two said it was their ambition to help their people. One boy returned my question, 'What do you think of the adivasis?'

The previous night, there had been a raid on the village by customs and police. About thirty men were detained, including the fathers of some of the children in this class. There has been a long history of gold-smuggling along the coast; and the largest haul of drugs ever taken in India was discovered near here last year. Tribal people had been used to conceal the large package of heroin. The smugglers were never caught.

Winin Pereira points out that the school gardens are full of imported and exotic plants: African marigolds, geraniums, dahlias. Just beyond the compound, the fields are full of wild flowers, plants and shrubs. He asks 'Why don't you grow what is familiar to the children in the school gardens? Why don't you find out the fruits and berries and roots which they eat?' The teachers themselves do not often appreciate the indigenous, the homely and the locally grown; their teaching itself has its origins in the distant, the imported, knowledge that is produced elsewhere. Pereira has been analysing the textbooks in use in the school: the life they evoke is overwhelmingly urban, industrial and Western.

He insists that rescuing traditional knowledge from the oblivion to which formal education would consign it is not an exercise in nostalgia, but a quiet search for political alternatives to industrialized, monetized patterns of development, an alternative that celebrates the local and the sustainable, prizes the human above material resources. That the European ecologists should have 'discovered' that all living creatures are interdependent, and that they, in turn, depend upon the non-living parts of the universe, he regards with wry detachment; after all, the adivasis have always known this. 'Conscientization' he says, 'is not only, or indeed, principally, for the poor.'

A year later, the Warli adivasis of the area protested, Chipko-style, against the felling of natural forest trees. The government of Maharashtra, ostensibly committed to forest conservation, nevertheless needs the revenue to be had from contractors who buy the timber and they permitted them to take a certain coupe of trees. When the contractors arrived, they were met by a thousand tribal people, who clung to the trees to prevent them from being cut. The concern of the Warlis was not for an abstraction called 'the environment', but with their own survival. 'Jungle bachao, manao bachao' was the slogan of the Kashtakari Sanghatana — save the forest, save the people. Deforestation has already degraded the living conditions of thousands of tribal people in the area; and to make matters worse, those who have always lived in balance with the forest are being accused of causing the damage. They are being stigmatized as 'encroachers', criminalized and blamed for the spoliation of the forests that have nurtured them, and which they have nurtured, for 4000 years. It is the bitterest spectacle, that the living examples of such hopeful and precious instruction in the meaning of sustainable social and economic practice should be in the way of being crushed into oblivion by the imperatives of the market economy.

The removal of the rich, organic diversity of the natural forest, and its replacement by monocultures of teak or subabul has profoundly wounded the lives of the adivasis. It has meant not only the loss to them of hundreds of species of trees that supplied them with renewable materials for housing, food, for manure, but has robbed them also of plants used for both medicine and food. Marginal farmers who had lived on a tiny parcel of ground, supplementing their diet with fruits, tubers and produce of the forest, have been doubly affected: the removal of trees erodes the land, because the fall of the monsoon rains is no longer broken by the dense foliage, and, secondly, for several years now the amount of rainfall has been decreasing. As a result, a field that gave five sacks of jowar five years ago now gives barely two. Paddy that yielded six sacks gave only three after last year's erratic monsoon. At this time of year — the adivasis burn the fallen leaves of the forest on their paddy-fields for fertilizer: every night the sky is red with fires. Teak leaves are less easily absorbed by the soil, and teak does not allow the traditionally rich vegetation to flourish in their shade. With the impoverishment of this natural growth, the tribals also lose their remedies for sickness, stomach ache, jaundice, scorpion and snake bites, fevers and cuts, which the forest supplied, and they must turn to allopathic medicines which are not only expensive, but which frequently involve, buying back traditional remedies neatly packaged by transnational corporations.

In the substitution of the monoculture of a single species

for the sheltering habitat of the adivasis, we can see a metaphor for a worldwide process sometimes dignified with the word 'development.' For the diversity of all traditional cultures is being extinguished in the monoculture of money, a mutation in which human beings become the most lucrative cash-crop of all. People are the highest-yielding variety ever conceived, and even though they require certain expensive inputs, they bear much of their own cost, and reproduce themselves. And so much of the crop can be exploited: So many qualities, powers, attributes that can be converted into commodities and sold back to them: the potential for bringing to market, for harvesting, for monetizing is unlimited. People are grown for profit like any other natural resource, the most raw material of all, infinitely pliable, adaptable. In this process, all the services that human beings can freely render each other, all the things that we can do for ourselves outside of the monetary system are derided and disgraced. The real crime of the adivasis is that they have resisted full entry into the market economy, and retain too much of an alternative way of living, which threatens the totalizing monoculture of the markets.

The paintings of the Warlis are much admired, and hang on the walls of the well-to-do in Bombay, Hamburg and London. (There was an exhibition of Warli art in London last year, and every item found a ready buyer.) In their art, they celebrate the symbols and significant objects of their daily life, the stylized shapes of the palms, the trees that give food and shelter — the timbrun, karoti, padal and kodi, — and where their hira dev (green god) lives, the sweet resins and secretions of the forest that nourish and give meaning. At the same time as we market their art, we are also willing their annihilation, for the same market system requires their trees for the paper, rayon, furniture and construction industries. In some areas, the people have migrated to the cities, to squat there in squalor and despair; others are corroded by alcohol, that destructive consoler for loss of balance with the natural world.

181

Where the forest remains, even in this, the dry hot season, it seethes with a multitude of life-forms that are absent from the silent plantations of teak and khair. Golden orioles, bulbuls, drongos, sunbirds and herons dart between the blossoms of the flame of the forest and the crimson silk-cotton flowers, langorous sulphur-coloured and dusty-blue butterflies hover on the sweet blooms of the common karvanda thorn-bush, the bark of the trees secretes its mysterious fragrant gum; at night, the fireflies wink at each other, and the cry of the jackals sets the dogs of the village barking excitedly all night long.

In India, the ancient sages retired to the forest in search of wisdom. Their understanding was that without a respect for all things, both living and inanimate, human beings cannot develop fully. Respect for the 'panch mahabhutas', the five elements which sustain all life — earth, water, light, air and space — is of great antiquity. The unquiet life of the late twentieth century makes it more urgent than ever that the retreat into the forest should remain possible. Yet what wisdom should we find in the barren monocultures, other than the reflection of our own inner desolation?

If you wish to receive *regular information* about *new books*, please send your name and address to:

London Bible Warehouse
PO Box 123
Basingstoke
Hants RG23 7NL

Name...

Address ....

....

....

....

I am especially interested in:
☐ Biographies
☐ Fiction
☐ Christian living
☐ Issue related books
☐ Academic books
☐ Bible study aids
☐ Children's books
☐ Music
☐ Other subjects